THE
NURSING HOME
CHOICE:
How to Choose
the Ideal Nursing Home

by

Marian R. Kranz, P.T.

BRANDEN PUBLISHING CO.
Boston

Library of Congress Cataloging in Publication Data

Kranz, Marian R.
  The nursing home choice : how to choose the ideal
nursing home / by Marian R. Kranz.
      p. cm.
  Includes bibliographical references and index.
  ISBN 0-8283-2030-6 (alk. paper)
  1. Nursing homes--Evaluation.
  2. Nursing home care--Evaluation.
  3. Consumer education.
      I. Title.
RA997.K72   1998
362.1'6--dc21   97-40534
                                          CIP

BRANDEN PUBLISHING COMPANY
17 Station Street
Box 843 Brookline Village
Boston, MA 02147

To Michael,
whose love and support made this book possible.

Contents

Preface

At some point in our lives, each of us will face the heart-wrenching task of choosing a nursing home for a parent, grandparent, or spouse. This book is designed as a step-by-step guide for making that important decision. Its primary purpose is to provide the general reader with the information necessary to choose a nursing home of exceptional quality. The material is presented in a user-friendly format for easy reading and comprehension.

Terminology used by professionals in the nursing home industry and in government regulations are printed in bold letters on the first usage and repeated frequently so the reader gains a familiar understanding of their usage. All examples used in this book to illustrate and further explain pertinent points have occurred exactly as they are written, only the names have been changed.

Rehabilitation services weigh heavily in the content of this book since these services and professionals are integral to the residents' improvement and recovery. In addition, these services are billed to Medicare and other insurance carriers separately from the general nursing care leaving these services open to numerous fraudulent practices from a variety of individuals.

Each chapter contains a brief overview to orient the reader to the material included in the chapter and a chapter summary to reiterate the major points. In addition, the information contained in each chapter builds upon the material of previous chapters to prepare the senior citizens, their family and friends to take an educated tour of a nursing home and to make an informed choice.

The intent of this book is to inform the reader about nursing home care. It is intended to be used by those considering placing themselves or a loved one into a care facility. As in any business, you will find the exceptional, the borderline, and those to be avoided. Those facilities whose care is exceptional and above reproach will have employees who answer your questions honestly in order for you to make an educated nursing home choice. These are the buildings you should seriously consider in your decision.

A few nursing home employees might recognize themselves or their questionable business practices as being brought to light, and may take exception to its content. In this situation, it is the hope of this author that the level of care they provide to their residents will be raised to match or exceed that of the best facilities.

Chapter 1
The Heart Wrenching Situation

T his chapter describes the history of nursing homes. It also illustrates a common accident which triggers the nursing home dilemma.

History of Nursing Homes

Nursing homes have existed for hundreds of years, primarily as a storage facility for society's undesirables. This group of unfortunates included the mentally impaired, physically infirm, and those with needs beyond the capabilities of their families. These institutions were filthy and overcrowded; the staff was insufficient and incompetent; the residents were neglected and abused. These abhorrent conditions stimulated a drastic change in the laws and regulations governing such facilities. All nursing homes are required to comply with these changes in the construction and safety of the building, the number and skills of the staff, and the care of the residents. However, some institutions have escaped the scrutiny of the governing agencies and continue to operate in this offensive manner. These nursing homes have become particularly creative at avoiding the regulations and the enforcement of those regulations to the extent that it becomes difficult to distinguish a quality nursing home from a poor one. Therein lies the nursing home dilemma.

Most Common Situation

Your aging father fell last week and broke his hip. The surgeons at the hospital repaired the hip but it will require several months to heal properly. The doctor informed you that your father cannot put any weight on that leg for at least two months. He has not been successful using a walker and must use a wheelchair. On your last visit, he was awake but seemed confused. The hospital bookkeeper informed you that he can stay until the end of the week at which time Medicare will stop paying his hospital bills. What are you going to do? What are your options? He could go home but your mother is in poor health also. She cannot care for him by herself. You and your spouse both have jobs so you are only available on evenings and weekends. The only alternative seems to be a nursing home.

This is an agonizing decision which each of us will have to face sooner or later. This decision is made more grueling by stories in the media of abuse and neglect running rampant in our nation's nursing homes. The employees of such establishments have even been filmed beating residents. It is not surprising that we agonize over this decision. However, in some situations, a nursing home is the only alternative. Choosing the right nursing home is the challenge.

Chapter Summary

Nursing homes have existed for centuries as a warehouse for individuals considered undesirable or unmanageable suffering from a variety of physical and mental ailments. Living conditions in these institutions were deplorable at best. Through the passage of federal and state laws, all nursing homes were required to make the necessary changes to improve the care of the residents. However, the administration of many nursing homes seem to enjoy the challenge of avoiding these laws with no regard for the residents. This savvy makes the task of choosing a quality nursing home a difficult one.

An accident such as the fall of a loved one, can place anyone in the predicament of making the nursing home choice at any time. The pressure of the discharge deadline enforced by Medicare adds to this dilemma and increases the need for guidance.

Chapter 2
Where to Begin

T his chapter introduces several sources of information and discusses the reliability of each. You will learn how to compile a list of **nursing home candidates** for the selection process based on objective criteria. Finally, this chapter teaches you the first criterion, Location, and how it is used to shorten your list of candidate nursing homes.

Sources of Information

Nursing homes are not the most popular topic of conversation. Most of us avoid this topic whenever possible. However, there are many sources of reliable information available to you. With this information a list of nursing home candidates will be compiled. This list should include the name of the nursing home, address with zip code, and telephone number. The following resources are immediately available.

Friends and Relatives

The first source of information includes your friends and relatives. Ask them if they have any experience with nursing homes. You may be surprised how many of them have been in the same situation. Word-of-mouth is, in many ways, an excellent source of truthful information, so ask them:

- What is its name?
- Where is it located?
- What did they like about it?
- What didn't they like about it?
- What were the deciding factors for their choice?
- Do they know other reputable nursing homes?
- Do they know anything about these other nursing homes?

The nursing homes recommended by your friends and relatives will begin your list of candidate nursing homes.

Hospital Discharge Planner

Another valuable reference is the hospital **discharge planner**. This individual is the hospital employee whose job is to assist the family in making arrangements for the patient's accommodations after they leave the hospital. This person (or persons) *should* be actively involved in the discharge of all patients. Ask the following questions: Is there is a particular nursing home to which they frequently discharge patients?

- Is there is a nursing home they would recommend?
- Why do they recommend this particular nursing home?
- These nursing homes should be added to your list of candidates for consideration.

Although the hospital discharge planner should be the ideal reference for nursing home information, a word of caution must be interjected. In some instance there exists an arrangement between the hospital and a nursing home for patient referrals. In this relationship, the hospital agrees to send their patients to this nursing home and the nursing home agrees to send their residents back to that hospital whenever they become ill. This exclusive relationship creates a financial incentive for the hospital discharge planner to limit your information in favor of their "preferred" nursing home. In fact, some discharge planners will make all of these arrangements with their preferred nursing home without consulting the patient or family. This manipulation violates the individuals' right to free choice, violates the professional ethics of all health professionals, and should not be tolerated.

Referral Services

Nursing home referral services store information on numerous facilities by geographic location. This information is supplied to them by the nursing home itself and is a marketing tool used by many nursing homes to increase their exposure to the public. Therefore, the information is biased and should be considered suspect. The referral service may also receive financial compensation from the nursing home for each referral. This establishes a financial incentive for the referral service to market the nursing home in its most positive light rather than provide objective information to the public. This suspicion of false advertising raises many legal concerns which are beyond the scope of this book.

Yellow Pages

The most comprehensive information source available to you can be found right in your own home. It is your local telephone book. The "Nursing Homes" section of the yellow pages will reveal a list of nursing homes in your area. Add these to your list of candidates.

The List

Now that you have compiled a list of nursing home candidates, the process of elimination begins. With each step, unacceptable nursing homes will be eliminated from the list as they fail to meet objective criteria. The first and simplest criterion is *location*.

Location

Think of this nursing *home* search as buying a house for yourself. As every home-buyer knows, the three most important things to remember about any piece of real estate is location, location, location. This is also true for nursing homes. Location should be the prime consideration regarding the nursing home for your loved one. Are you looking for a nursing home which is close to your home or close to your place of employment? The important issue here is that the nursing home must be conveniently located for you to visit frequently. Frequent visits will be vital to the health of your loved one, so weigh these options carefully. Will you visit more frequently if they live close to your work or close to your home?

With that decision made, exclude from your list any facilities which are not located within a reasonable driving distance. If any of these nursing homes cannot be visited conveniently, cross them off your list. If you are unsure of the location of any of them, include them. Their actual location can be verified later.

Using the street address of each nursing home, plot its location on a map of the area. This will require a detailed map which includes side streets and residential areas.

Are any of these nursing home candidates too far away to allow for convenient visits? If the answer is yes, strike them from your list. The result is a list of candidates which is considerably shorter each of which is within an acceptable driving distance.

Chapter Summary

There are many sources of reliable and objective information which can be accessed in order to compile a list of candidate nursing homes. Friends and relatives are the most truthful sources of information. The hospital discharge planner is a valuable reference if the credibility is untainted by financial incentives in favor of preferred nursing homes. Referral services possess vast quantities of information organized by geographic location. This information should be considered biased since it is provided to them by a nursing home staff member and may include financial incentives for each referral. The most comprehensive source of objective information is the yellow pages of the local telephone book.

From these sources, a list of candidate nursing homes has been compiled and the elimination process begins based on objective criteria. Location, the first criteria, is determined through personal knowledge of the area and plotting the nursing homes on a detailed map. All candidates located outside the acceptable driving distance are eliminated.

Chapter 3
Telephone Interviews

N ow that you have shortened your list of candidates by their location, you are ready to contact those remaining nursing homes. You will learn how to conduct these interviews and what questions to ask. Each of these questions is discussed in detail including answers which indicate their compliance with federal and state laws and regulations. This chapter also teaches you how to evaluate their answers for false information using real-life examples.

Interview Questions
Conducting telephone interviews is a time-efficient method for obtaining necessary information by which to further reduce your list of candidate nursing homes. As you telephone the first candidate on your list, your call will be answered by the staff member who is closest to the telephone at that time.

During your conversation with this random staff member, listen closely to the words they use to answer the telephone and their tone of voice. Did the telephone ring incessantly before it was answered? Did they answer the telephone in a professional manner? Do they seem willing to answer your questions or do they make you feel as if you are imposing upon them and their day? Are you left on hold for an extended period of time? These indicators will reveal in the first few seconds the level of professionalism among the staff.

Your target for this preliminary interview is the administrator or the director of nurses. Inform them that you are interviewing nursing homes for a possible admission and ask them the following questions:

1. Who owns the nursing home?
2. Is it privately owned or corporate owned?
3. Is the nursing home **Medicare certified**?
4. How many Medicare-certified beds do they have?
5. How many residents *can* they have living there?
6. How many residents *do* they have living there?
7. Is there a waiting list?
8. How many people are on staff?
9. How many of those staff members take care of the residents?
10. Is there a **physical therapist** on staff?
11. How many days per week is **physical therapy** provided?
12. How many days per week is occupational therapy provided?
13. How many days per week is **speech therapy** provided?
14. How many days per week is **restorative nursing care** provided?

What Do They Mean?

1. Who owns the nursing home?
2. Is it privately owned or corporate owned?

The ownership of the nursing home is important to the care provided within the building because within the latitude of State regulations, the owner sets the standard of care for each specific nursing home. The owner decides whether to obey the state investigators or launch a legal challenge. For instance, a large corporation owns a nursing home which failed to comply with several of these regulations on their last **state survey**. That corporation is able to use its attorney to challenge those regulations which they failed to satisfy. A letter from the corporation's attorney threatening legal action will usually suffice.

A large corporation has the capital to make this legal challenge and the state survey process is not able to withstand the financial onslaught of litigation. Therefore, this letter of challenge is placed in the nursing homes' **plan of correction** and the violations are ignored. The purpose of these regulations is to ensure the health and proper care of our elderly. However, if they can be easily challenged by a ruthless corporation, they are ineffective and the elderly patient suffers the consequences. This also establishes the dangerous precedent that if nursing home owners are ruthless and wealthy, they can violate state and federal law without fear of retribution.

On the other hand, a large corporation which truly cares for its residents, will have more professional consultants at its disposal. Among these will be nursing consultants for the nursing staff, rehabilitation consultants for the therapists, and dietary consultants for the cooks.

The privately owned nursing home is uncommon but a few remain in operation. These nursing homes typically do not have the financial resources to legally challenge the regulations so they must comply with them or go out of business. They also, do not have the supply of

consultants available to support their staff with specialized expertise. Therefore, the resident who requires
extremely specialized care will not receive it. However,
the residents know the staff on a first-name basis and
there is a lower rate of staff turnover. These two factors
result in better general care for the residents.

3. Is the nursing home Medicare certified?

If your loved one has been in the hospital for at least
three days, he/she probably qualifies for Medicare **coverage** and may need a Medicare certified nursing home.
This way, Medicare will cover the cost of their care. If
this nursing home is not Medicare certified, Medicare
will deny the insurance claims for the care of its residents. If the answer to this question is yes, this nursing
home remains on your list. If the answer is no, mark
them off your list.

4. How many Medicare certified beds do they have?

Medicare certifies a certain number of beds in each
nursing home and this number varies from one nursing
home to another. Medicare will cover the cost of nursing
home care to all residents assigned to one of these
Medicare certified beds provided they meet all other
criteria. For example, Pleasant Valley Nursing Home has
20 Medicare certified beds and all of them are full, but
they have two vacancies in the non-Medicare section.
Peaceful Meadows Convalescent Home has only 15
Medicare certified beds but two of them are vacant.
Peaceful Meadows has no other vacancies at this time.
Regardless of the vacancies in other sections of the
building, Pleasant Valley Nursing Home should be

marked off your list since all of their Medicare certified beds are full. Peaceful Meadows Convalescent Home, on the other hand, should remain on your list since they have two vacant beds in their Medicare section. Simply stated, if you are looking for a nursing home at which Medicare will cover the cost, your loved one must be assigned a Medicare certified bed. If all of the Medicare certified beds in this building are occupied, mark this nursing home off your list.

5. How many residents *can* they have living there?
6. How many residents *do* they have living there?

These two questions will tell you their total **census** for which they are licensed and their current census. If their current census is low, there is a problem with the care they are providing. Ask them why they have such a low census? Their answer will include a variety of excuses ranging from the believable to the completely outrageous. However, the actual reasons for a low census include: Poor results on a state survey; **Stop Placement** status; high death rate; high rate of discharges back to the hospital.

The first two reasons refer to the state survey process and will be discussed in their entirety in chapter five. The third reason, high death rate, is self explanatory. If there has been a high number of deaths at this nursing home, mark them off your list immediately. Admitting your loved one to this kind of facility may result in an agonizing death in the very near future.

Reason number four, High rate of discharges back to the hospital, is another indicator of poor care. If a multitude of residents have required hospitalization recently, they were neglected. A low census is a reliable indicator that something is wrong. If you suspect a problem, strike them off your list and move on.

Of equal concern is the nursing home whose current census exceeds their possible census. Each state grants operating licenses to nursing homes within their borders to care for a specific number of residents. To exceed that number is a direct violation of state law. If you encounter such a nursing home, not only should you mark them off your list but report this crime to the state authorities for further action.

7. Is there a waiting list?

If the answer is yes, how long is it? Hospitals will frequently set a discharge deadline, a date by which the patient must be moved to a nursing home. If this nursing homes' waiting list is lengthy (weeks or months), this building will not be able to meet the hospital's discharge deadline so mark them off your list. However, the hospital may be flexible (within a day or two) if they know you are actively searching for a facility. Consult with the Discharge Planner. It is their responsibility to administer the Medicare regulations for the benefit of the patient.

8. How many people are on staff?
9. How many of those staff members take care of the residents?

The total number of people on staff will include those who care for the residents directly, such as nurses and therapists but it will also include the **support staff**, such as cooks and housekeepers. The answer to question nine will break this down by giving you the number of staff members in **direct patient care**. Included will be nurses, nurses' aides, physical therapists (**PT**), occupational therapists (OT), speech-language pathologists, and **restorative nursing aides** (**RNA**).

Pay close attention to the staff-to-resident ratio. This term refers to the number of staff in direct care of the residents compared to the number of residents and is calculated from the answers to questions six and nine. The number of staff caring for each resident must be high for adequate care to be provided 24 hours per day. For example, Oakridge Convalescent Home boasts of having a total staff of 128 to care for 100 residents. However, the number of care-giving staff is only 100. Therefore, there is only 100 staff members providing direct care to l00 residents around the clock, a 1 to 1 ratio. Pleasant Valley Nursing Center has a direct care giving staff of 200 to care for 100 residents. This equates to a 2 to 1 ratio or 2 care giving staff for every resident. Clearly, Pleasant Valley Nursing Center is better staffed.

While the **staff to resident ratio** refers to the number of care-giving staff for each resident, it does not use the total number of staff since to do so would include housekeeping, maintenance personnel and office staff. Such an inclusion would mislead you into thinking that there were more staff caring for the residents than is actually the case.

10. Is there a physical therapist on staff?

The PT may be an employee or a contractor. While the employment status of the PT is of less importance than their availability, an employee is available throughout the day whereas the contractor is not.

Medicare regulations require each nursing home to provide skilled **rehabilitation services** including physical therapy, occupational therapy, and speech-language pathology services. The nursing home must provide these services to all patients who require them or risk losing their Medicare certification.

Physical therapy is an indicator of the status of the entire rehabilitation department. If physical therapy services are not available, this nursing home is in violation of Medicare regulations, so strike this building off your list. If physical therapy is available, occupational therapy and speech-language pathology is probably be available also. However, there are no guarantees. Some nursing homes provide physical therapy services but fail to provide the other **rehab** services. The dishonest administrator will attempt to coerce the PT into providing occupational or speech therapy services for which she is not qualified. This situation is discussed in detail in chapter six. Since their services are required by Medicare, if an occupational therapist or a speech-language pathologist is not available, mark this nursing home off your list.

11.   How many days per week is physical therapy provided?

In the nursing home setting, physical therapy seeks to improve the strength, coordination, and ease of movement of the patients' arms and legs. Physical therapy also attempts to improve the residents' ability to walk; OR If they are permanently in a wheelchair, works to improve their ability to propel the wheelchair themselves. In this way, the residents live as independently as possible at whatever level they **function**.

In order for a nursing home physical therapy department to be successful, the PT must be present a minimum of five days per week. Residents whose care is covered by **Medicare Part A** are eligible for skilled physical therapy services a maximum of **twice daily, five to seven days per week**. Residents whose care is covered by **Medicare Part B** are eligible for skilled physical therapy services a maximum of **once per day, five days per week**. According to state regulations, the nursing home must provide or make available all rehabilitation services required by the resident. Therefore, physical therapy services *must* be available on a regular and frequent basis. If this is not the case, cross this nursing home off your list and move on.

12. How many days per week is occupational therapy provided?

Occupational therapy seeks to improve the activities of daily living which most of us take for granted, such as dressing, grooming, and personal hygiene. The occupational therapist also consults for the nursing staff in developing restorative nursing care programs to prevent further decline of those abilities. As mentioned above, state regulations require that the nursing home provide or make available all rehabilitation services which are required by the resident. Therefore, occupational therapy services *must* be available. If not, strike this candidate from your list.

13. How many days per week is speech therapy provided?

Speech therapy seeks to improve the resident's speech and **cognition**. The term "speech" refers to the ability to speak clearly. "Cognition" refers to the ability to think clearly: to take in information, process it in their brain, and to respond to it using words or actions. While these skills are taken for granted by most people, they are vital to our participation in society. These skills are also affected, either temporarily or permanently, by many medical conditions, such as stroke, Parkinsonism, Alzheimer's disease, and surgical anesthesia.

In addition to speech and cognition, the Speech/Language Pathologist (**SLP**) is trained to identify problems the resident may experience swallowing food or liquids. Problems with swallowing often result in choking or death. This dysfunction can also lead to aspiration, a condition in which the food or liquid goes into the lungs instead of the stomach. Aspiration frequently leads to lung infections and pneumonia, which are often fatal in senior citizens.

If you have any concerns regarding your loved one's speech, cognition, or swallowing make sure the SLP addresses those needs. In addition, state regulations mandate that speech therapy, as a rehabilitation service, be made available to those patients who require it. Therefore, if speech therapy is not available, cross this nursing home off your list.

14. How many days per week is restorative nursing care provided?

Restorative nursing care should be provided at least once per day, seven days per week in order to achieve the goal of maintaining the patient's current functional abilities. Ideally, a resident is evaluated by a skilled rehabilitation professional: the physical therapist, the occupational therapist or the speech-language pathologist. This professional designs a restorative nursing program specific to the resident's needs, completes any necessary training of the RNAs and periodically monitors that patient's status. Unfortunately, this situation is rare. The more common scenario is that a **nurses' aide** decides that a resident needs a restorative nursing care program. This nurses' aide shares her opinion with the charge nurse who, in turn, orders the RNA to put that resident on a restorative nursing care program. The RNA, as ordered, makes up an exercise program for the resident with no evaluation or consultation with any of the appropriate rehabilitation professionals. The following is a specific example of this.

Mrs. Smith fell in her room today but escaped injury. Her **nurses' aide** decided that her fall was a sign that she needed a walker. Upon hearing this opinion, the charge nurse ordered the RNA to give Mrs. Smith this assistive device. The restorative nursing aide found a few old walkers in a closet in the rehabilitation department and chose one at random. No one answered her knock at Mrs. Smith's bedroom door, so this RNA placed the walker just inside the room and left.

There are many problems with this example. The reason for Mrs. Smith's fall was not identified. What was she doing when she fell? What kind of shoes was she wearing? Has she been ill recently? Have her medications been changed recently? Was she wearing her glasses? Was her balance affected? Was her strength affected? These are just a few of the areas which must be addressed by a skilled physical therapist. The results will illuminate the reason for Mrs. Smith's fall. If she does need a walker, the type, size and adaptations are critical to her safety. Obviously, this resident suffered by receiving sub-standard services from the nurses' aid, the charge nurse and the RNA. None of these individuals are qualified to evaluate Mrs. Smith or address her need for ambulation devices. The only person qualified to do this is the PT.

In the example above, it is the responsibility of the physical therapist to evaluate Mrs. Smith's condition and initiate a skilled physical therapy program if necessary. If a restorative nursing care program is indicated, the PT designs the program including any equipment, instructs all appropriate staff members, and periodically monitors Mrs. Smith and her program.

While Mrs. Smith was being treated by the PT, her therapy is covered Medicare. However, her restorative nursing care program is not covered by Medicare. A brief rule of thumb is that skilled therapy services include physical therapy, occupational therapy, and speech-language pathology and are covered by Medicare Part A and Medicare Part B. Health **maintenance** services, such as restorative nursing care programs, which do not require a skilled professional are not covered by Medicare Parts A or B.

In order for Mrs. Smith's therapy to be covered by Medicare Part A, her condition must require the skills of a licensed therapist and the services must be provided at least once per day, five days per week. If either of these criteria are not met, Medicare Part A will deny Mrs. Smith's insurance claim. The answers to questions 11-14 will indicate if this nursing home provides therapy services according to these Medicare regulations.

One final point: Some nursing homes have an SLP on a contractual basis, to perform swallow evaluations without addressing the resident's need for speech therapy or cognition training. Therefore, when asked if speech therapy services are available, the nursing home representative may answer truthfully in the affirmative when only swallow evaluation are performed. This nursing home completely neglect these two areas, speech and cognition, which are so vital to a complete recovery following a stroke. If your relative has suffered a stroke, it is imperative that the nursing home employs or contracts with an SLP who can address all of their needs not just their swallowing.

Chapter Summary

Telephone interviews, targeting the administrator or director of nurses of each nursing home, reveal valuable information necessary for this elimination process. This interview begins as the telephone is answered by paying close attention to the manner in which the staff member answered the telephone.

Corporate-owned facilities have greater financial resources to provide better support for the staff and better care to the residents or to utilize violate federal and state regulations without fear of retribution.

In order for Medicare to pay the bills for your loved ones care, they must be in a Medicare-certified bed within a Medicare-certified building. The current census should approximate the capacity of the nursing home without exceeding it. A lengthy waiting list eliminates this facility from your list without need of further interviewing. This nursing home is not able to meet your deadline.

The staff-to-resident ratio refers to the number of staff members caring for each resident. This number should be high in order to provide adequate care to all of the residents.

Medicare regulations, as well as federal and state laws require that Physical Therapy, Occupational Therapy and Speech Therapy services be provided to all residents who need them. Residents who are covered by Medicare Part A are eligible for skilled therapy services twice daily, five to seven days per week. Residents who are covered by Medicare Part B are eligible for services once daily, five days per week. Restorative Nursing Care should be provided seven days per week.

The administrator or director of nurses should know the answers to all 14 questions. As a potential customer and family member of a potential resident, you have the right to have all of these questions answered completely. The nursing home administration may not want to share this information, but you have the right to know. If the answers to any of these questions raise serious concerns or if the administration refuses to provide an acceptable answers, cross this nursing home off your list.

In order to take an educated tour of the first nursing home on your list, you will need a working knowledge of Medicare and Medicaid insurance programs which will pay for the care of your loved one and the State Survey process which regulates the operation of nursing homes.

Chapter 4
Medicare and Medicaid

T his chapter focuses on the basics of Medicare and Medicaid regulations as they apply to nursing homes and their residents. In this chapter, you will learn how to determine **entitlement** and **eligibility** for both Medicare Part A and Medicare Part B insurance coverage. Special attention is given to skilled therapies under Medicare and Medicare reimbursement caps. Medicaid regulations as they pertain to nursing home residents are also discussed. Pertinent points are further illustrated by diagrams and flowcharts.

Basic Medicare

Medicare has the reputation of being a tangled web of confusing regulations. This reputation has been earned through the myriad of regulations one must decipher in order to gain even a basic understanding of the insurance coverage. This confusion is further compounded by the frustration we experience when dealing with this government-run insurance "company". But, once broken down, this jumble of regulations actually makes sense.

As many people are already aware, Medicare is regulated by the federal government. Its purpose is to provide health insurance to those citizens who meet all of their requirements. What many people don't know is that the Medicare program is administered by private insurance companies. These insurance companies, one of which is Aetna, have contracts with the Medicare agency to administer the Medicare program. So when you send an insurance claim to "Medicare", you are actually sending it to one of these **intermediary** insurance companies which are commonly referred to as **intermediaries**.

There are two types of Medicare coverage, Medicare Part A and Medicare Part B. Medicare Part A is *Hospitalization* coverage, and this is what most people refer to when they use the term "Medicare". Medicare Part B, on the other hand, is *Medical* coverage for outpatients. This will be discussed in detail later.

Medicare Part A

Medicare Part A covers Hospitalization. To receive Part A coverage, you must meet the requirements for *entitlement*. To be entitled to receive Medicare Part A coverage you must be included in one of the following categories:

You are 65 years of age or older
You have been disabled for more than two years
You suffer from end-stage renal disease
You suffer from black lung disease
You are a railroad employee

Most people qualify for Medicare Part A coverage by being 65 years old or older. However, someone younger than 65 years of age may be entitled to Medicare Part A coverage if they have been diagnosed by a physician as being disabled. Two years after that diagnosis is made they may apply for Medicare Part A coverage. This would include any young person who is disabled as a result of an accident or illness.

Those who suffer from end-stage renal disease are also entitled to Medicare Part A coverage. This is the last phase of a fatal kidney disease. Other groups who qualify for Medicare Part A include anyone who has black lung disease or has been employed by a railroad. Figure 1 presents a flowchart illustrating these entitlement criteria.

After satisfying any one of these requirements, you are awarded a Medicare Part A card which entitles you to 100 days of skilled nursing care in a hospital or nursing home. This 100 day counter begins upon admission to the hospital and continues as you are discharged from there and admitted to a nursing home.

For the first 20 days of that 100 day allotment, Medicare Part A pays 100% of the cost of your care. For day 21 through day 100, Medicare A pays 80%, leaving the remaining 20% to be paid by your co-insurance. This 20% can add up quickly so it is very important to have co-insurance. Figure 2 summarizes Medicare Part A coverage broken down by day.

Now that you possess your Medicare Part A card which identifies your entitlement to Medicare Part A *coverage*, you must meet the requirements for "eligibility" for this particular illness. This is referred to as the **spell of illness**. There are two basic requirements for eligibility to receive Medicare Part A *benefits* for this illness. You must either have a three day stay in the hospital, or be admitted to a nursing home within thirty days of the last Medicare Part A covered day in a hospital or other nursing home.

This three day stay in the hospital is ambiguous in that different hospitals count the days differently. Some hospitals write down the exact time of admission and discharge to calculate precisely three 24-hour periods.

Figure 1
Flowchart illustrating entitlement requirements

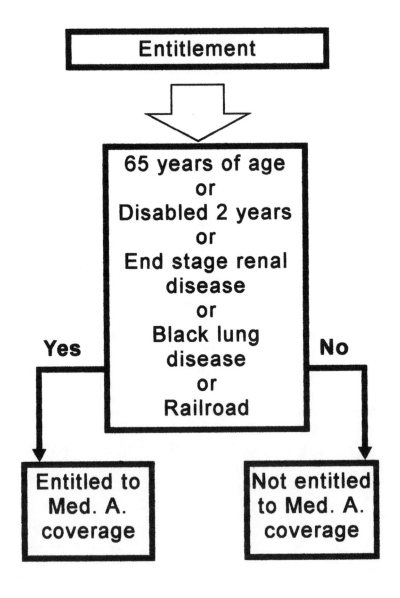

Figure 2
Medicare Part A Benefits By the Day

ILLNESS	BENEFITS
Days 1-20	Medicare covers 100% of cost.
Days 21 - 100	Medicare covers 80% of cost. The remaining 20% is the responsibility of your secondary insurance, which may cover some or all of the remaining 20%, depending on your policy.
Days 101 and above	Medicare covers 0%. Secondary insurance covers costs according to your policy.

With one 24-hour period being one day, this method calculates the three day hospital stay to the minute.

Other hospitals use the simpler method of counting the number of midnights. Using this method, a patient qualifies for Medicare Part A coverage after being in the hospital for three midnights regardless of the time of day at which they were admitted or discharged.

The discrepancy between the methods used by different hospitals to administer these Medicare requirements is a concern. Medicare claims will be paid or denied based on the method used to calculate the three day hospital stay. For example, Mr. Downs is admitted to Newport Medical Center at 2:00pm on Monday and discharged at the usual discharge time of 10:00am on Thursday. Since Newport Medical Center calculates the three day hospital stay by counting midnights, Mr. Downs' hospital stay qualifies him for Medicare Part A benefits and his hospitalization is fully covered.

It is fortunate for Mr. Downs that he was admitted to Newport Medical Center instead of Jones County Hospital across town. Since Jones County Hospital tracks admissions and discharges to the minute, his hospital stay would not qualify him for Medicare Part A benefits and his insurance claim would be denied leaving him with a monstrous bill. Figure 3 illustrates this discrepancy and its effect upon the patient.

The alternate requirement for Medicare Part A eligibility for this spell of illness states that you must be admitted to a nursing home within 30 days of the last **Medicare covered day** in a hospital or other nursing home. This 30 day window of opportunity for those patients, who try living at home after a hospitalization, may find that they need extra care which cannot be provided at home. They can still seek admission to a

Figure 3
Discrepancies between two methods of calculating
the 3 day hospital stay for Medicare A eligibility.

NEWPORT MEDICAL CENTER	JONES COUNTY HOSPITAL
Counts number of midnights regardless of time of admission or discharge.	Calculates specific time of admission and discharge for three 24 hour periods.
Mr. Downs stayed:	Mr. Downs was admitted:
Monday night +	At 2:45 p.m. Monday and
Tuesday night +	Discharged at 10:00 a.m. Thursday
Wednesday night =	Totalling 2 days, 20 hours.
Eligible for Medicare A	NOT eligible for Medicare A

nursing home within 30 days of their discharge from the hospital and the cost of their care will be completely covered by their Medicare Part A insurance coverage. Their 100 day allotment will continue counting from the day of their hospital discharge as if they were admitted directly to a nursing home and never went home at all.

Another use for this is the patient who is admitted to a nursing home and does not use their entire 100 days before returning home. If that patient finds that they went home too soon, they can be re-admitted to the nursing home within 30 days of their discharge. All of their care will be covered by their Medicare Part A benefits for the remainder of their 100 day allowance as if their attempt to return never occurred. The flowchart in Figure 4 summarizes these eligibility requirements.

Included among the Medicare Part A benefits are specialty services, which encompass all of the skilled rehabilitation services in the hospital and in the nursing home. Among these skilled rehabilitation services are physical, occupational, and speech therapies. Once the criteria for entitlement and eligibility have been satisfied, these services may also be covered. However, skilled therapies have an additional set of coverage criteria. Those requirements are:

Therapy services must be required daily or two times per day, at least 5 days a week.

Therapy services must require the skills of a licensed therapist.

Therapy cannot be done on an outpatient basis.

There must be documentation of a recent loss of **mobility** or function

Figure 4
Medicare A eligibility requirements

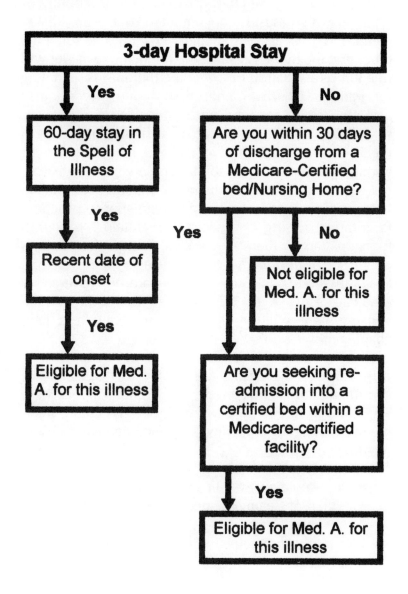

While each of these requirements must be met, the last one is the most important. In order to be considered an appropriate candidate for rehabilitation services, the patient must have suffered a *recent* loss of mobility or function which must be *documented* by a licensed staff member. This licensed staff member should be someone other that the therapist, since the Medicare reviewer will rule this as a situation in which the therapist is searching for patients to treat rather than treating those who actually require her services.

Services which are not covered by Medicare Part A include general supportive care for maintenance or **endurance**, and any rehabilitation service which does not require the skills of a licensed therapist. Restorative Nursing Care is an example of a maintenance program. Restorative nursing care seeks to *maintain* a resident's function rather than *improve* their function and is performed by *unskilled, unlicensed* personnel. Therefore, Restorative Nursing Care programs are not covered by Medicare Parts A or B. The specifics of Restorative Nursing Care will be discussed in detail in a later chapter of this book.

If your loved one is receiving therapy under Medicare Part A coverage, there should be considerable documentation in the medical chart to support these services and to ensure payment by the Medicare intermediary insurance company. This documentation should include:

- An evaluation by a licensed physical therapist
- A plan of treatment specific for that patient
- Weekly progress notes
- Monthly summaries of the patients condition and progress.

- A discharge summary at the time of discharge from the skilled therapy program.

If any of these items is missing from the medical chart, the therapist treating the patient and the facility are in violation of federal and state regulations. In addition, this claim will be denied payment, leaving the patient and his/her family with an enormous bill.

One final use regarding the 100 day allowance of Medicare Part A coverage--One hundred days is ample time for any necessary applications to be completed for Medicaid or other financial resources. If your loved one is planning to remain in the nursing home, you have 100 days to complete the applications and make any other financial arrangements to qualify for the Medicaid program. The Medicaid program is discussed in more detail later in this chapter. Alternative financial assistance programs are available and should be investigated.

Medicare Part B

Medicare Part B is *Medical* coverage. It differs from standard medical insurance in that it is sold only through the Social Security Administration (SSA). As with any insurance company, the SSA requires an application for coverage. If your application is accepted, you are entitled to Medicare Part B insurance coverage. The coverage is unlimited and is dependent upon the need for services. The beneficiary must pay a monthly premium with an annual deductible. If Medicare Part B is the **primary** insurance, it pays 80% of all charges considered by the reviewer to be **reasonable and customary** once the deductible is met. The co-insurance pays the remaining 20%. If Medicare Part B is the **secondary** or **co-insurance**, it pays 80% of the portion of the bill which the

primary insurance did not pay. For example, Mrs. Platt is covered by Medicare Part A as her **primary** insurance and Medicare Part B as her **co-insurance**. Her total bill was $1000.00. Medicare Part A paid 80% of the bill which is $800.00 leaving a balance of $200.00. Since her deductible was already met, Medicare Part B paid 80% of that remaining bill with a payment of $160.00. This left only $40.00 for Mrs. Platt to pay out of her own pocket. The diagram in Figure 5 illustrates this insurance coverage.

The above example applies to situations in which the patient is covered by both Medicare Parts A and B for days 21 through 100 of their allotted 100 days of coverage. Remember that Medicare Part A coverage changes during the course of those 100 days. Therefore, the amounts paid by each of these insurance programs will change as well. Figure 6 illustrates the combination of Medicare Part A as primary with Medicare Part B as co-insurance and how this coverage changes during the 100 day Part A period.

Part B Failures

As with Medicare Part A insurance, Medicare Part B has its own set of criteria for entitlement and eligibility. Once you have met the entitlement criteria for Medicare Part B insurance coverage, you may be eligible for Medicare Part B benefits for this spell of illness. In order to be considered eligible for Medicare Part B benefits for this illness, you must have suffered a **change in condition** or an **exacerbation**/flair-up of symptoms without requiring a three day hospital stay. The three day stay would qualify you for Medicare Part A (Hospitalization = 100 days) coverage assuming you met the entitlement criteria.

Figure 5
Diagram illustrating Total Out-of-Pocket expenses when combining Medicare A and Medicare B

Explanation	Expenses
Total bill	$1000
Medicare A pays 80%	($800)
Remaining 20%	$200
Medicare B pays 80-% of this remainder	($160)
Total Out of Pocket	$40

Figure 6

Combination of Medicare A as Primary and Medicare B as Secondary, broken down by day.

DAY	MEDICARE A	MEDICARE B
1 thru 20	Covers 100%	Covers 0%
21 thru 100	Covers 80%, leaving 20% for secondary insurance	Covers 80% of the 20% which Medicare A didn't pay
101 and beyond	Covers 0%	Covers 80%

Those nursing home residents who suffer an actual change in condition without a three day hospital stay are frequently not identified as candidates for rehabilitation services. One reason for this oversight is that the therapist is in the building for only two or three hours per day and is completely unaware of their change in status. In this case the therapist relies heavily upon the nursing staff for information. However, communication between the nursing and therapy staffs is nonexistent, or at best, riddled with bickering and petty jealousy. The first reason for this strained relationship is turf-guarding. Until recent years, the PT has been an infrequent visitor to the nursing home, with the nursing staff enjoying complete control and authority over the care of the residents. However, with the increase in geriatric physical therapy, the nursing staff has been forced to share that control.

Turf-guarding is coupled with resentment toward the individual therapist serving their nursing home. These nurses feel a deep need to protect "their" residents from all outsiders. They feel very possessive of their residents and resent any interference by the therapist or other professional.

The last two reasons strike at the professional nature of geriatric nursing and geriatric physical therapy in a nursing home. Geriatric nurses feel that their residents have worked hard during their lives and deserve to rest during their twilight years. They view their role as caregiver to their residents, providing for every need until that resident dies. Geriatric physical therapists, on the other hand, view their role as one of improving the resident's strength and vitality; To assist the resident in becoming as independent as possible for the remainder of their lives. These two roles are opposite in their professional focus and in their goals for the residents.

The final reason for this conflict between the nurse and the therapist is that the ultimate goal of the PT is to discharge the patients back to their homes. This practice results in empty beds which the nursing home administrator will fill with new admissions. This cycle of admission and discharge is the ultimate goal of the nursing home. However, it creates additional paperwork which is not particularly appreciated by an administrative nursing staff.

Ideally, the nurses and therapists should work together for the benefit of the patient. Some nursing homes operate in this fashion but they are rare and easily identified. These nursing homes will have a high rate of discharging patients back to their own homes outside the nursing home.

Therapy Services Under Medicare

It is the responsibility of the skilled rehabilitation professional, specifically the PT, occupational therapist, or SLP, to ensure to the best of their ability that the resident meets all criteria for entitlement and eligibility prior to initiating a skilled evaluation. The rehab professional must be familiar with, and knowledgeable regarding, the Medicare Part A and Medicare Part B insurance programs in order to administer these benefits in the best interest of their residents. Unfortunately, many of these rehabilitation professionals are not familiar with these regulations. Therefore, it becomes necessary for the patient or a family member to acquaint themselves with this information to ensure that they receive the benefits for which they have paid. For this reason it is important to review Medicare Part A and Part B regulations as they apply to skilled rehab services.

Medicare A Therapies

Rehabilitation services include physical therapy, occupational therapy, and speech therapy. These services are provided by licensed PTs, OTs, and SLP, respectively. The regulations for Medicare Parts A insurance coverage list several criteria which must be met in order to qualify for skilled rehabilitation services.

The patient must reflect a recent change in **functional status**, such as they are no longer able to walk under their own power; they are no longer able to get out of bed by themselves; or they can no longer push their own wheelchair. This functional change is usually evident since this patient must also have a three day hospital stay.

The patient must have a treatment diagnosis or condition which indicates a need for rehabilitation services, such as a broken bone, surgery, or a recent loss of walking ability.

The treatment diagnosis or condition must have a **recent date of onset**. This term, date of onset, means the date when this condition began or when the surgery or accident occurred. The term, recent, is somewhat ambiguous since there is no regulation which defines this time frame. It is left to the discretion of the claims reviewer who reviews that particular claim. Since there is no definite time frame written in the regulations, the best approach is to call the claims reviewer and ask them for their interpretation of this issue. This individual will make the ultimate decision of whether this claim will be paid so it is best to go directly to them for this information. The claims reviewer can be reached through the Medicare customer service and claims department whose telephone number is on the patient's insurance card.

All rehabilitation services must be properly documented. This required documentation is listed below:

- Prescription or order from the physician
- Skilled evaluation from the therapist
- Plan of treatment specifically designed for that patient
- Weekly progress notes
- Monthly summaries of the patient's condition and progress for that month
- Discharge summary of entire course of treatment

All of this must be enclosed in the resident's chart. This medical chart is the property of the resident and as the resident's family member or legal representative, you have the right to view this medical information. Although the nursing home administration will discourage this, you also have right to arrange for this chart to be reviewed by an independent medical reviewer. This review is completed outside the nursing home with a photocopy of the medical chart. Expect to pay a nominal copy fee.

Upon receiving the photocopy of the medical chart, verify that the entire chart was copied. This can be done quickly and easily by comparing the thickness of the copy to the thickness of the original. If there is a discrepancy between the thickness of these two documents bring this to the attention of the administrator immediately and contact the Department of Health in your state. This is a clear violation of your rights and the rights of your loved one. In addition, remove your loved one from this nursing home immediately. This attempt to hide information is an indicator of numerous violations of federal and state regulations which are lethal to the residents.

The services must be skilled in nature and must require the skills of a licensed therapist. If the services could be performed safely and effectively by an untrained and unlicensed individual, they will not be covered. For instance, the **physician's order** for Mr. Donovan reads "to encourage walking around the nursing home to improve endurance". This does not require the skills of a licensed therapist and would not be covered. Mr. Sanders, on the other hand, does require the skills of a licensed therapist. He suffered a number of falls recently and one of those falls resulted in an injury to his ankle. There were no broken bones but he requires strengthening exercises and instruction in walking with a cane, as well as balance training to avoid additional falls. His physician's order read "Strengthening exercises, balance, and use of a cane." Since this treatment requires the skills of a licensed therapist it would by covered.

The services must be needed once or twice per day, five days per week. If the services are needed only three times per week, they could be performed on an outpatient basis and would not be covered by Medicare Part A. However, they could be covered by Medicare Part B.

The services required or the patient's condition must be such that they can only be provided on an **inpatient** basis. They must be extensive and complex enough to require admission to the hospital.

The patient must have rehabilitation potential and make significant progress in a reasonable and predictable period of time. The patient must demonstrate to the therapist that they have the potential to improve in their functional abilities and that there is a good chance they will achieve their functional goals in a reasonable period of time. In order for Medicare to pay for rehabilitation services, there must be consistent and measurable progress. Each week the therapist must observe progress in the resident's condition and document that progress in the weekly progress note. That progress must be measurable on an objective scale such as the distance the resident is able to walk or the number of pounds the resident is able to lift. This progress must also be linked to a functional goal such as Mr. Johnson is able to walk 25 feet with his walker and verbal cues 50% of the time. The dining room is 50 feet away from his room in the nursing home.

The order or prescription from the physician must include the procedures to be performed, the frequency at which they will be performed, and the duration for which they will continue. The order cannot read simply "PT 2 times per day until relieved". A correct order will read: "PT to include Hot Moist Packs, Ultrasound, Therapeutic Exercise, and Body Mechanics Training, Daily, 5 days per week for 3 weeks". This order includes what procedures the therapist is to perform, how many times per day, and for how many days. If one of these elements is missing from the treatment order, the Medicare claims reviewer will deny the claim resulting in nonpayment from the insurance carrier.

All of the above mentioned criteria must be met in order to be considered a candidate for rehabilitation services under Medicare Part A. If any of these criteria is not met, the patient is not an appropriate rehab candidate. If a patient receives rehabilitation services without meeting all of these criteria, the claim is at risk for denial and nonpayment. Figure 7 summarizes these requirements.

Medicare Part B Therapies

Medicare Part B lists many of the same requirements as Medicare Part A. However, there are a few differences. Once you have met the *entitlement* and *eligibility* requirements for Medicare Part B, the following criteria must be met in order to be considered an appropriate candidate for rehabilitation services. Of the requirements listed above for Medicare Part A, the following also pertain to Medicare Part B.

1. The services must require the skills of a licensed therapist. If these services can be adequately performed by a lesser skilled member, medicare will not pay for the service.

2. The patient must reflect a **recent change in func tional status**. For Medicare Part B, the term "functional status" refers to the patient's ability to take care of himself as well as their ability to get around at home and in the community. In order to receive therapy under Medicare Part B, a resident must suffer a recent change in their ability to perform these activities. For instance, a patient who uses a wheelchair functions at a different level than a patient who walks but this, alone, does not qualify the wheelchair-bound patient for therapy services. However, if that patient became wheelchair-bound recently, they would qualify.

This change must be recent. As with Medicare Part A the term "recent" is not specifically defined in the regulations. It is usually left to the Medicare claims reviewer to make this determination. In the past, a good

Figure 7
Requirements for Therapy under Medicare A

Requirements:
"Inpatient" status =3 day hospital stay.
Required services must be skilled in nature.
Services must require skills of a licensed therapist.
Recent change in functional ability.
Rehab diagnosis with a recent date of onset.
Services must be required 5 days per week.
Patient must have rehab potential.
Physician's order must include precedures, frequency, and duration.
Patient must make significant progress in a reasonable and predictable period of time.
Proper documentation.

rule of thumb has been that if this change in status occurred within the last two months, the patient qualifies for therapy services under Medicare Part B. However, as cutbacks are made in the Medicare system, these ambiguous criteria for coverage are being tightened.

In some parts of the country this rule of thumb has been narrowed to thirty days or less, so a good recommendation is to telephone the claims reviewer in your area and ask for their interpretation of this issue. This individual can be located at the customer service and claims department of the Medicare intermediary whose telephone number can be found on the patient's insurance card.

3. The rehab services must be provided on a daily or less than daily basis, five times per week or less. If the patient's condition is complex enough to warrant rehab services more than five times per week, they should be covered under the Medicare Part A program, not the Medicare Part B program.

4. All documentation must be complete. This requirement states that the plan of treatment must be certified and re-certified by a physician every 30 days in order to continue treatment. This is usually accomplished when the therapist completes a monthly summary and sends it to the physician for their review and signature.

The key here is that this must be completed every 30 days, not monthly. The physician's signature on this document must be dated within 30 days of the previous certification. Since there are more that 30 days in some calendar months, re-certifying a patient monthly is not frequent enough. This violates the regulations and will result in denial of the claim.

It is the responsibility of the therapist to complete the appropriate documentation in a timely manner, allowing time for mail delivery. After this form is completed, it is the responsibility of the clerical staff to send it to the physician. This step in the process must also be completed in a timely manner. If this form sits on someone's desk or in someone's IN box for a few days, the 30 day requirement will not be satisfied and the claim is at risk for denial.

5. The patient must have rehab potential and make significant progress in a reasonable and predictable period of time. There are actually two components to this criteria. The first is that the patient must have potential to be rehabilitated. The therapist must be able to recognize this potential and determine the period of time required to achieve it.

Recognizing the patient's rehabilitation potential is completely dependent upon the skills of the licensed therapist and is the fundamental reason why only a licensed therapist can perform this duty. The state licensure process guarantees a minimum skill level. If a therapist did not have at least those minimum skills, she would not pass the state licensure exam. However, among the group of licensed therapists, there is a wide range of skills. Some therapists are more skilled in one specialty area while the expertise of other therapists lie in other areas. Even within the specialty of **geriatrics**, different therapists have specific areas of expertise. For example, one therapist may specialize in treating wounds, such as bed sores, while another therapist may specialize in treating stroke patients.

This is similar to medical doctors who specialize in a particular field of medicine. No one would expect a cardiologist to perform orthopedic surgery. The same clinical specialties exist among therapists. However, all therapists should be able to recognize the rehab potential of their patients. In addition, if the patient's condition is outside the therapist's area of expertise, she is obligated by state law to refer the patient elsewhere.

The latter part of this criteria states that the patient must make significant progress in a reasonable and predictable period of time. This is another reason for the skills and experience of the therapist. She must be familiar enough with the condition of the patient and with the insurance regulations to accurately predict that patient's progress. She must document this expected progress in the form of treatment goals with a deadline for achieving each goal. Once documented, those goals must be achieved by the patient. If one of these goals is not achieved, an acceptable reason such as an unexpected illness or injury, must be documented.

6. The treatment order or prescription must include procedures, frequency, and duration. It is the responsibility of the therapist to ensure that the treatment order includes all of these areas in order to comply with Medicare Part B regulations. If the treatment order does not include all of this information, the insurance claim for this therapy program may be denied.

Figure 8 summarizes these regulations and Figure 9 illustrates the differences between these two insurance programs in the coverage of rehab services.

Justifications for Medicare Part B

Medicare Part B insurance coverage is often purchased as secondary insurance to Medicare Part A. This combination allows Medicare Part B to pick up where

Figure 8
Requirements for Therapy under Medicare B

Requirements:
"Outpatient" status = No 3 day hospital stay.
Required services must be skilled in nature.
Services must require the skills of a licensed therapist.
Recent change in functional ability.
Recent date of onset.
Services required 5 days or less per week.
Patient must have rehab potential.
Physician's order must include procedures, frequency, and duration.
Patient must show significant progress in a reasonable and predictable period of time.
Plan of treatment must be re-certified every 30 days.
Properly documented.

Figure 9
Diagram comparing Medicare A requirements to Medicare B

Medicare A Inpatient	Medicare B Outpatient
Services at least 5 days/week	Services less than 5 days/week
	Certified / Re-certified every 30 days
Skilled services	
Licensed therapist	
Recent change in functional status	
Recent date of onset	
Rehab potential	
Physician's order includes procedures, frequency and duration	
Patient must show significant progress in reasonable and predictable period of time	
Properly documented	

Medicare Part A leaves off to provide complete coverage for the patient. For this to occur, the patient's specific situation must justify Medicare Part B coverage.

60 Day Stay in the Spell of Illness

This criterion affects the hospital or nursing home patient entitled to Medicare Part A but cannot satisfy one of the requirements for eligibility. This patient is not eligible for Medicare Part A benefits during this spell of illness, but Medicare Part B may be justified.

This situation occurs when a patient has numerous complications requiring frequent hospitalizations. The Medicare regulation pertinent to this situation is referred to as the **60 day stay in the spell of illness**. This regulation means that there must be at least 60 days between hospital visits in order to qualify for Medicare Part A. For example, Mrs. Smith is admitted to the hospital with a heart condition. Five weeks ago, she was in the hospital for her diabetes. The second hospital stay is covered by Medicare Part A because there was only 35 days between these two hospital visits instead of 60 days, as required. However, Medicare Part B coverage may be justified.

Exhausted 100 Days

Another justification for Medicare Part B occurs when a hospital or nursing home patient has exhausted their allotted 100 days of Medicare Part A coverage. This patient may be justified in continuing their rehabilitation services under Medicare Part B benefits. These are usually cases of catastrophic conditions such as a stroke or amputation. Regardless of their need for continued services, it is more common for this inpatient to be discharged from their therapy program on day 101 whether they are functionally ready or not. Although, this policy violates insurance regulations, as well as state laws governing the practice of physical therapy and the operation of nursing homes, it is a common cost-cutting mechanism. This will be discussed in detail in chapter 6.

Exacerbation of an Existing Condition

This jargon refers to an illness or injury that suddenly gets worse. If this exacerbation results in a change in functional abilities, rehab services are justified under Medicare Part B. In this situation, it is crucial that this change in functional abilities is identified. In reality these residents and their condition change are over-looked by the nursing staff. The PT or OT is unaware of the resident's change in condition since they are in the building only two or three hours per day. This results in a gradual and continual decline in the resident's health, until their death.

Ancillary Benefits

The term *ancillary* refers to benefits itemized sepa-rately as a part of the insurance package. These benefits are covered in addition to the standard cost of care. It is also cost-driven, which means Medicare reimburses the provider, usually the nursing home for their billed amounts. Typically, there is an exorbitant mark up of these costs in an effort to make more money. These ancillary benefits are as follows:

- Outpatient rehabilitation
- Primary surgical dressings
- X-rays
- Prosthetic devices such as artificial limbs
- Hip replacements

- Lab work
- Physician visits

The first five services on this list are billed to Medicare by the nursing home. Lab work is billed by the laboratory which provided this service and physician visits are billed by the physician.

Medicare Reimbursement caps

When a nursing home gains certification to provide health care services in the Medicare program, that nursing home signs a contract with the Medicare intermediary. Each intermediary is an insurance company that, in turn, contracts with the Medicare agency to administer the Medicare insurance program.

This contract between the nursing home and the insurance intermediary includes a daily, per patient **reimbursement rate** for Medicare Part A which the nursing home will be paid for providing all necessary services including nursing and rehabilitation. This rate is essentially a cap, meaning that it serves as a maximum amount the nursing home will be paid per day for that patient. If the cost of the services for a particular patient exceeds this reimbursement rate, the nursing home is *not* paid for that excess. Therefore, it is vital for the nursing home to consider all of the necessary services when negotiating the daily, per patient reimbursement rate or they will lose money.

For the patient who suffers from a complicated illness or injury which requires extensive nursing and rehabilitation services, the daily cost of their care may exceed this cap. For example, Mr. Johnson suffered a severe stroke and is admitted to a nursing home. That nursing home has a reimbursement rate of $100 per patient per day.

Mr. Johnson requires extensive nursing care and rehabilitation services including physical therapy, occupational therapy and speech therapy to regain his **functional independence**. The cost of all of these services is $145 per day, but the insurance company will only pay the nursing home $100 per day. The extra $45 is a daily loss to the nursing home. Obviously, if this occurs too frequently, the nursing home will be in serious financial difficulties.

THEN, THEY MUST CUT COSTS ELSEWHERE.

Cutting Costs

Nursing home administrators use a variety of methods to cut costs. A few improve staff efficiency; most jeopardize the health and well-being of the residents.

Refusing Complex Patients

The first method is to refuse to admit patients with complicated problems. This is accomplished through deception. The administrator informs the patient's family that the nursing home "cannot meet the needs of this patient". By using this terminology, it appears that the nursing home administrator is looking out for the welfare of this patient and confessing honestly that their needs are beyond the skills of his staff. The truth is that this nursing home has a low reimbursement rate and would lose money if they admitted complex patients such as Mr. Johnson.

Premature Discharge from Therapy

If complicated patients such as Mr. Johnson are admitted to the nursing home, the administrator may elect to limit the financial burden by having him discharged from therapy services before he is functionally ready. As soon as he is discharged from therapy, the short-term cost of his care is decreased. However, the cost of his long term care will be greater since he will not be able to do anything for himself. The cost of 24 hour nursing care for the rest of his life is staggering. If therapies are provided immediately, he stands a better chance of regaining much of his independence and possibly be discharged. Unfortunately, we will never know because a shortsighted administrator could not look beyond the immediate reimbursement cap of $145.

Staff Reduction

Down-sizing the number of **certified nurses' aides** or **CNA** on staff is a common method of cutting costs. Since the primary responsibility of a CNA is the daily care of the residents, reducing their numbers is a decrease in the direct care givers of the residents. This increases the number of residents to each CNA, thus increasing the workload of each CNA and increasing the resident-to-CNA ratio. The result: poor care.

Another staff member targeted for cost-cutting lay-offs is the **bath aide**. A bath aide is a CNA whose sole responsibility is to bathe the residents. If the number of bath aides is decreased, then the number of residents bathed each day is decreased. Therefore, the residents are not bathed as frequently as they should be, resulting in poor hygiene, frequent illness, and an increased rate of infections.

Reduction in Work Hours

A more drastic measure used by administrators, involves cutting the work hours of all of the staff. This has ramifications throughout the building. The number of CNAs and bath aides are cut, as in previous methods, but the hours of the licensed nurses are affected as well. The medication nurses have a shortened work day is shortened so they have to work faster, resulting in an increased risk of medication errors. The work day of each charge nurse is shortened resulting in incompetent supervision of the CNAs who, themselves are already overworked. Even the kitchen staff suffers from shortened hours so the quality and nutritional value of the meals also suffers. The housekeeping and maintenance departments are no longer able to keep the building and equipment clean and in good working order. This drastic measure affects all aspects of the residents' lives from their personal care and hygiene, to the quality of their food, and to the safety of the roof over their heads. In fact, in 1991 the roof did collapse in one western Washington nursing home.

Breach of Contract

This tactic involves avoidance or even blatant refusal to pay a contracted therapist for services rendered. Despite the signed contract between the administrator and the therapist, it is common for the administrator to refuse to pay the monthly bill. Besides putting a prompt end to the business relationship, the therapist has only two options: Write it off as a business loss; or File a civil suit. Most therapists elect the first option since the nursing home and its corporate owners have the financial resources to stage long and very expensive litigation.

Medicaid

Most individuals who enter a nursing home will not be able to return to their own homes. This is the reality. It is also a reality that the cost of medical care for these residents is staggering and getting higher every day. Therefore, Medicaid must be addressed as a financial option. The one hundred days of Medicare Part A coverage allows time to investigate the criteria for qualifying for Medicaid assistance. It is the responsibility of the nursing home social worker to do this for you or at least provide assistance. However, like other staff members, the social worker has a large caseload and reduced work hours so DO NOT RELY ON THEM TO DO THIS.

To qualify for Medicaid there is a maximum financial limit of liquid assets or "money in the bank" which the patient cannot exceed. Put simply, your loved one cannot have a large sum of money. If they do, they must pay for their own care before Medicaid will assist them. This is referred to a **spend down**. If they have no living spouse and own their home, they may be required to sell the property and use the proceeds to pay for their care before they can qualify for Medicaid. If their spouse is living in the home, there is no requirement to sell. The social worker and discharge planners employed by the hospital and nursing home should be familiar with the specifics for Medicaid. Ask for their assistance BUT DO NOT RELY ON IT.

Chapter Summary

Medicare Part A provides hospitalization coverage for those who meet entitlement and eligibility requirements. This inpatient coverage begins upon admission to the hospital and continues with admission to a nursing home for a maximum of 100 days. Every citizen who is at least 65 years of age is entitled to Medicare Part A.

Medicare Part B is governed by the Social Security Administration and requires a premium and deductible like most insurance programs. Many of the eligibility requirements applicable to Medicare Part A also are pertinent to Medicare Part B.

Rehabilitation services under Medicare are dependent upon the therapist identifying the resident as a rehab candidate. There are many reasons why residents are overlooked for rehab services, among them are: Absence of the therapist; and Lack of knowledge of Medicare regulations.

Medicare Part B insurance coverage may be purchased as a secondary insurance plan to Medicare Part A. This complete insurance package allows Medicare Part B to pick up where Medicare Part A leaves off. The specific justifications for this include the 60 day stay in the spell of illness, exhaustion of the allotted 100 days, and exacerbation of an existing condition. Medicare also covers a number of ancillary benefits which are billed and paid for, in addition to the general cost of caring for the resident.

To join the ranks of Medicare certified providers, a nursing home must sign a contract with an intermediary insurance company for a maximum reimbursement rate. This caps the amount the insurance company will pay the nursing home for caring for each resident. If the nursing home administrator fails to negotiate a sufficient rate to cover all of the needs of the resident, the nursing home will lose money. Strategies used by administrators to cut costs include refusal to admit complex patients, premature discharge from therapy, staff reduction, and breach of contract through refusal to pay for services rendered.

The 100 days afforded to every Medicare Part A patient provides a safety net to allow family members time to investigate other financial assistance mechanisms such as Medicaid. If the patient possesses any note-worthy assets, a spend down may be required before Medicaid will lend any assistance.

Chapter 5
OBRA and The Survey Process

T his chapter focuses on the Omnibus Budget Reconciliation Act and the impact of this reformation on the operation of nursing homes. In this chapter, you will learn how the state governments have succeeded in enforcing these federal regulations and how they have failed. Special attention is given to the state survey process in its attempt to enforce these regulations.

OBRA

In 1987, the US Congress passed the Omnibus Budget Reconciliation Act, commonly referred to as OBRA '87, or simply OBRA. This act consists of a set of regulations to be implemented by each State and enforced through the State survey process. The term "survey process" refers to the method in which state investigators examine the operation of a nursing home for competency. This examination is intended to enforce these regulations.

The OBRA guidelines completely reformed nursing home requirements so they would focus more on **resident outcomes**. The focus of nursing home written policies and procedures shifted toward the care and well-being of the residents. However, some state surveyors who are responsible for monitoring the nursing homes for compliance and for enforcing these regulations are easily distracted with other issues and need frequent reminders to redirect their attention back to their new goal: Improved **resident outcome**.

The term "resident outcome" means the effect of an action on the resident. In determining this effect, the surveyor contemplates a series of questions. Did the action harm the resident in any way? Did the lack of action harm the resident in any way? Did the action interfere with the resident's progress in any way? Did the lack of action interfere with the resident's progress in any way? For example, a state surveyor enters Mrs. Anderson's room at 4:00 PM. A foul odor is pungently obvious. Mrs. Anderson is sitting in a wheelchair by the window with her bare feet resting on the cold tile floor. She is still wearing her nightclothes; her glasses and hearing aids are on a shelf above the bed. This obvious neglect of the resident is all too common in nursing homes. This lack of care would be considered by the state surveyor to be harmful to Mrs. Anderson and an interference with her medical care. This incident would be reported to the charge nurse immediately for prompt attention to Mrs. Anderson's needs. When the survey team completes the **survey report** of this nursing home, this incident will be included on the list of citations.

As demonstrated in the above example, the focus of the state surveyors has shifted toward resident care. As a part of this focus, the survey process requires extensive interviews of those residents who are considered interviewable, so the residents themselves have the opportunity to inform the state surveyors about their care.

Under the OBRA regulations, the interdisciplinary care plans have become the focus of the state survey. As a primary component of each resident's medical chart, the care plan must reflect an integrated outline for the resident's care with contributions from each of the involved health professionals. These documents must be updated whenever the resident undergoes a change in their health or living situation, such as an illness, a fall or a room change. However, since illness and falls occur on a daily basis in most nursing homes, the required documentation is usually ignored.

This is especially true in the case of someone who falls frequently. Mr. Adams, for example, suffers from Alzheimer's disease and suffers frequent falls, once or twice each day. Each time he falls, the CNA helps him back to his room and into bed. An hour or so later, the charge nurse visits him to check for broken bones. There is no examination of pulse or blood pressure. There is no documentation of the fall. There is no investigation of the reason for his fall or any precautions taken to prevent subsequent falls.

The following scenario illustrates the proper procedure for a fall. Upon finding Mr. Adams on the floor, the CNA calls to a fellow staff member to alert a charge nurse. Without moving Mr. Adams from his position, the CNA takes his pulse and blood pressure. The charge nurse examines Mr. Adams for injuries as well as taking additional pulse and blood pressure before moving him. If the results of this initial examination are negative, he is assisted into a wheelchair and transported to his room where a more thorough examination is performed. Mr. Adams' family should be notified as well as his doctor. This entire incident should be documented in his medical chart and some States require each fall to be reported to the Health Department. In most instances, none of these required procedures are followed.

In addition to updated care plans, OBRA requires that all nursing homes have a **Registered Nurse (RN)** on the day shift, seven days a week, and an RN or a **Licensed Practical Nurse** or **LPN** as Charge Nurse during each shift. In reality, most nursing homes, employ an LPN for the position of Charge Nurse, relying on the Director of Nurses with the standard 8:00 AM to 5:00 PM work day, to satisfy the requirement for an RN. This suspicious scheduling warrants close examination.

Like hospitals, most nursing homes divide the 24 hour day into three 8 hour shifts. These shifts are scheduled 7:00 AM to 3:00 PM, 3:00 PM to 11:00 PM, and 11:00 PM to 7:00 AM. The OBRA regulations require an RN to be on duty during the day shift, which actually includes the 7:00 AM to 3:00 PM shift and the 3:00 PM to 11:00 PM shift. Therefore, the Director of Nurses who works the standard 8:00 AM to 5:00 PM work day cannot satisfy this regulation. The shortcut commonly used to avoid this regulation is to refer to the 7:00 AM to 3:00 PM shift as the "day shift" scheduling an RN as charge nurse for that shift only. An LPN is then scheduled as charge nurse for the remaining two shifts.

State Survey

The State Survey process is charged with the task of enforcing the OBRA regulations. It is an extensive process which falls within the realm of the Health Care Financing Administration. A typical nursing home survey is conducted as follows.

On an annual basis, a team of state surveyors will enter a nursing home. This team generally numbers from three to seven individuals and consists of nurses, a maintenance inspector, and a dietary expert. Their primary function is to review the nursing home's methods of operation for compliance with OBRA guidelines and State regulations. This review includes, but is not limited to, all documented policies and procedures regarding the operation of the nursing home, medical care of the residents, qualifications of the staff, personal interviews with residents and families, a review of the medical charts and a review of personnel files. The state surveyors tour the nursing home, examine the structure for safety, observe the skills of the staff performing their duties, and conduct private interviews with the residents and family members.

A nursing home survey requires four to ten days to be completed and it becomes obvious when a nursing home is being surveyed since the first action of the survey team upon entering the facility, is to post a sign on the front door as notification that a state survey is in progress.

Plan of Correction

After the surveyors complete their review, they prepare a written report listing all of the Level A and Level B citations for this nursing home. The more citations, the thicker the document. The nursing home administration then prepares a **Plan of Correction** in response to the citations. This written response must include the corrective action described in detail, identify the responsible staff member, and specify any training needed by that staff member in order to effectively carry out this new responsibility. The necessary training must also be documented upon completion.

Every nursing home is required, by law, to have their last survey report and plan of correction available for the review of the public. If it is not available or if the administrator refuses a request to review this document, then he is violating yet another regulation.

Level A vs Level B Citations

During their review the surveyors examine the operation of the nursing home for compliance with the OBRA regulations. As mentioned previously, these regulations are subdivided into **Level A** and **Level B requirements**, with **Level A requirements** referring to the most serious and potentially life threatening issues while Level B refers to quality of life issues.

Level A requirements reflect issues of safety and residents' rights. An example of a safety violation is tap water which runs too hot out of the faucet. The risk of a scalding burn makes this an obvious safety hazard. An example of a resident's rights violation is forcing a resident to lie down for a nap after breakfast against their will. Another incident of this occurs in the dining room when a resident is force fed a meal they don't like. Forcing a resident to act against their will is a violation of their individual rights and freedoms guaranteed by the United States Constitution and is taken quite seriously by all state surveyors.

Failure to comply with Level A requirements could result in immediate closure of the building or being assigned **Stop Placement** status. This designation means the nursing home cannot admit any new residents until the infractions of these regulations are corrected, and the stop placement status is officially lifted by the state survey team.

Specialized Rehabilitation Services are the subject of many Level A requirement. One of those requirements states that a nursing home must provide or obtain rehabilitative services such as physical therapy, occupational therapy, and speech therapy for every resident it admits. In reality, only those residents who were recently admitted receive these skilled rehabilitation services. The needs of current residents for these services are over-looked.

This oversight occurs because these residents are not identified by the staff as qualifying for rehabilitation services according to Medicare and other insurance programs. There are many reasons for this failure. One reason is that the physical therapist, occupational therapist, and speech-language pathologist are in the building for only a few hours each day. They are not present to observe the resident's problem so they rely upon the nursing staff to keep them informed. The nursing staff is not educated in the justifications for therapy services so they do not realize when a resident needs therapy. The absence of the therapist combined with the lack of education of the nursing staff results in failure to provide necessary services to the residents.

This Level A requirement has a Level B companion requirement. The Level B states that if Specialized Rehabilitation Services are required in the resident's care plan, the nursing home must provide the required services or obtain the required services from an outside source. Therefore, if the resident's condition requires Specialized Rehabilitation Services, the nursing home must employ those professionals or arrange for those services to be provided by a rehabilitation contractor.

This Level B requirement also states that the nursing home is responsible for insuring that the services are provided in a timely manner by qualified personnel who meet all professional standards.

In spite of this requirement, physical therapy services are often provided by unskilled individuals who have no training and no license. The educational requirements of the physical therapy staff are covered in detail in the next chapter.

The Level B requirements also address the use of **restraints**. A restraint is any device placed on or around the resident to restrict their movement, such as belts or straps which the resident is unable to remove themselves. If the nursing home staff member uses a restraint on a resident, this Level B requirement mandates a detailed procedure which must be followed. There must be evidence documented in the medical chart of a consultation with appropriate health professionals, such as the physical therapist or occupational therapist. This consultation must include the use of less restrictive supportive devices, referring to any device which does not restrict the residents movements and is easily removed by the resident, such as pads or cushions. There must be a consultation with the resident's family informing them of the need for the restraint and the family's approval must be clearly documented. The last step in this procedure is a prescription from the resident's physician ordering a particular restraint to be used at a specified time of day for the resident's safety.

This entire procedure must be completed prior to the use of any restraint. Consider the following examples.

Mr. Dawson uses a wheelchair to get around and is unable to stand up by himself. For the last few days he has attempted to stand up by himself and has fallen during each attempt. Fortunately, he was not injured. The nursing staff alerted the PT who evaluated Mr. Dawson and his wheelchair. A cushion was adapted to Mr. Dawson's body proportions to provide support and comfort. The PT consulted with Mr. Dawson's family and the nursing home staff to educate all of them regarding the proper use of the cushion in his wheelchair. These consultations and training sessions were appropriately documented in Mr. Dawson's medical chart and an order was obtained from Mr. Dawson's physician prescribing the use of the cushion. Mr. Dawson made no more attempts to get out of his wheelchair without assistance.

In this example, Mr. Dawson did not need a restraint as he was uncomfortable. An appropriate cushion was used as a **less restrictive support device** to improve his posture and comfort in his wheelchair. This attention to the reason for his attempts to stand up, solved the problem without requiring the use of a restraint.

Like Mr. Dawson, Mr. Everett used a wheelchair to maneuver around the nursing home, was successful at it, and appeared satisfied with this mode of transportation. Then, one day he began standing up from his wheelchair by himself, an activity which is dangerous for him in his weakened condition. The PT was consulted. Over a short period of time, she made numerous adaptations to the wheelchair structure and cushions for improved support and comfort. She designed an exercise program in an attempt to improve Mr. Everett's strength, coordination, and balance in the attempt to re-train him to perform this activity with independence and safety.

Unfortunately, Mr. Everett was not unable to follow the simplest instructions. This therapist, then conversed with the physician and family members for any information they might have. However, in spite of these numerous attempts, Mr. Everett was still unable to stand safely and continued to make several attempts each day.

Having exhausted all alternatives, the therapist, physician, and family agreed that a **physical restraint** was necessary. These consultations were properly documented in Mr. Everett's chart along with a written prescription from the physician specifying the restraint to be used, the exact circumstances under which it may be applied and the duration of time which it can be left on.

Mr. Everett's situation outlines the appropriate procedure for using a restraint. A physical restraint was used only as a last resort with very specific guidelines for its application and duration of use. As demonstrated in this example, even if the therapist recommends a physical restraint, the situation must first be explained to the resident and family members or that resident's legal representative. If these individuals agree and the physician prescribes it, then the restraint device may be used. All of these consultations and conversations must be documented in the medical chart.

Although the law requires this multifaceted procedure for the use of restraints, they are often applied by the nurses' aide or a licensed nurse as they deem necessary, without prior consultation with the therapist, physician, or family. With no regard for the law or the resident, some nurses and nurses' aides use restraints for their own convenience or as a disciplinary measure. For example, if a resident makes frequent attempts to get out of their bed or wheelchair, the nurse will tie them down with a restraint. Those residents most at-risk for being restrained are those who tend to wander.

This procedure works well when utilized properly. However, there are some obstacles which must be surmounted. One obstacle is the absence of the therapist. For most nursing homes, the PT and OT are present only 2 to 3 hours per day, Monday through Friday. They are rarely present when an incident occurs in which a nurse or nurse's aide is tempted to use a physical restraint. Therefore, no therapist is consulted. In some instances, a **physical therapy assistant (PTA)** or restorative nurses' aide (RNA) is consulted. However, neither of these staff members is qualified to evaluate a situation of this kind. In fact, it is illegal for either the PTA or RNA to evaluate any resident, as it constitutes "practicing physical therapy without a license".

State regulations mandate the use of less restrictive support devices as an alternative to restraints. Another mandated alternative is a screening or evaluation by the therapist for rehabilitation services. A resident who has displayed a recent change in functional status may be an appropriate candidate for skilled rehabilitation services. However, the only way to determine this is for the PT or OT to screen or evaluate that resident. A screening is a quick assessment of the resident and the medical chart to determine if there has been a recent change in the resident's functional abilities. Unfortunately, in many buildings only Medicare Part A patients, recently admitted from the hospital, are seen by the PT or OT. Current residents are overlooked by the nursing staff and are unnoticed by the therapist as potential rehab candidates.

The continual problem of residents being overlooked for therapy services is rooted in the unavailability of the therapist, since she is only in the building a few hours each day. She simply is not there to address the needs of the residents as they occur and by the time she arrives the next day, the nursing staff has already mismanaged the problem. For instance, Mr. Gooding who is scheduled for an afternoon nap has already made five attempts to get out of bed this afternoon by himself. He was not injured but the charge nurse is completely frustrated with the situation and directs the CNA to apply a chest restraint to tie him down on his back. Since the PT left at noon, she is not there to address this problem and by tomorrow morning, the situation will be old news.

Another contributing factor to the therapist availability problem that some nursing homes have a different therapist each day so there is little **continuity of care** for the residents. This variety of therapists results from the failure of the nursing home to hire or even contract with their own individual therapist. Instead, the nursing home administrator signs a contract with a large therapy company to provide rehabilitation services.

These therapy companies employs many therapists to service their client nursing homes. Ideally, the therapy company assigns one of its therapists to service that client nursing home and its residents. However, this one-to-one relationship is a lofty goal which is seldom achieved. In reality, the client nursing home is passed around from one therapist to another depending upon which therapist has time to visit the nursing home on that particular day or depending upon which therapist will be in that geographic location on that particular day. The arrangement puts the nursing home staff in the uncomfortable position of not knowing who will show up or when to expect them. As the mystery therapist arrives at the building each day s/he is given a list of which Medicare Part A patients are to be seen that day. The result is that only recently admitted patients receive the attention they need. Current residents who may qualify for skilled rehabilitation services under Medicare Part B are overlooked, since the therapist is unaware of their existence.

Family Action

If you are not completely satisfied with the care of your loved one, there are several options at your disposal. The simplest is to address your concerns with the nursing home staff. Your first choice is the charge nurse.

If you are not satisfied with her course of action in resolving your concerns, discuss the situation with the Director of Nurses. If you are still not satisfied, consult the Administrator or the physician. By this time, your concerns will probably be addressed. However, if the problem continues, you have the option of contacting the Department of Health in your state. There is a toll free HOTLINE number for this purpose. This number should be posted near a pay telephone inside the nursing home. This is a requirement in most states. This number is also listed in the government section of your local telephone book. If the Department of Health has received other calls regarding this nursing home, there may be an investigation or an immediate State survey.

Changes in the Survey Process
Effective July 1, 1995, changes were enacted in the process of surveying nursing homes. The focus of these changes is to:

- Set minimum standard for substantial compliance
- Specify a broad range of remedies in response to noncompliance
- Establish guidelines for scope and severity in the enforcement of those remedies, and
- Discourage short term compliance

Although these changes went into effect July 1, 1995, the penalties and remedies portion of the new process are not yet in effect.

When this new survey process is fully effective, the Level A and Level B requirements will no longer exist. Substandard quality of care will be defined as one or more significant deficiencies in:

- Resident behavior and facility practices
- Quality of life
- Quality of care

A determination of substandard quality of care can include monetary penalties, up to $10,000 per day, effective upon identification of noncompliance with regulations, and for periods of past noncompliance. The severity of the deficiencies will be judged based on a scale ranging from **no actual harm with potential for minimal harm** to the resident, to **immediate jeopardy of the residents' health or safety.** The scale for assessing the scope of deficiencies ranges from **isolated incidents** to **wide-spread occurrences.**

The new survey process will also focus more closely on the nursing home's quality assurance program. A review of the quality assurance program is not a part of the old survey process unless the facility is under an extended survey.

Chapter Summary

In 1987, the US Congress passed the Omnibus Budget Reconciliation Act (OBRA) to reform nursing home operation requirements to focus more on resident outcomes. Did the action or lack of action harm the resident or interfere with their progress in any way?

As a primary component of the resident's medical chart, the interdisciplinary care plan has become a focus of the survey team in their review of the nursing home's operation. Although these documents are required to be updated with each fall or change in condition suffered by the resident, this mandate is rarely upheld. Staffing requirements mandated by the OBRA guidelines are also subverted through suspicious scheduling.

The State Survey process is charged with the task of enforcing these regulations and issuing citations against all violators. A team of state surveyors reviews the operation of each nursing home annually, submitting a written report to the nursing home administration listing all citations.

The administrator must submit a written plan of correction detailing the corrective action addressing each citation, the responsible staff member and all necessary training required for the safe and effective execution of that action.

State and federal law requires each nursing home to have their last survey report available for public review at all times.

OBRA regulations are divided into Level A and Level B regulations with Level A referring to safety and human rights issues and Level B referring to quality of life issues. Since a Level A citation designates a potentially life threatening situation, failure to comply with this level of regulation often results in stop placement status for the nursing home. This is a probationary status during with the nursing home is forbidden from admitting new residents until the life threatening problem is resolved to the satisfaction of the survey team. Only then is the stop placement status lifted.

Level B regulations address issues including rehabilitation services and restraints. The nursing home is required to provide all specialized rehabilitation services necessary for the optimal care of the resident. These services must be provided in a timely manner, by qualified personnel, and according to a physician's prescription. Restraints may be applied for the safety of the resident only after less restrictive support devices have been attempted, all appropriate consultations have been completed, all pertinent staff members have been trained, all documentation is in order, and according to the physician's prescription specifying the conditions and duration under which it may be applied.

If the care of your loved one is lacking, share your concerns with the charge nurse. If these issues are not resolved, consult the Director of Nurses; and if you are still not satisfied, consult the Administrator. If a resolution is not found, the problem is not an isolated incident but involves wide-spread occurrences and should be reported to the Department of Health in your state. There is a toll free HOTLINE number posted near the pay telephone inside the nursing home or it can be found in the government section of your local telephone book.

Effective July 1, 1995, changes were enacted to improve the state survey process. These changes will include stricter penalties and remedies for violations but this portion of the improvements is not yet if effect. When these changes are fully effective, substandard care will invoke monetary penalties of up to $10,000 per day. The actual amount will depend upon the severity of the violation, its potential for causing harm to the resident, and the frequency with which the incident occurred.

With a working knowledge of Medicare insurance coverage and the State Survey process, you are now ready to embark on an educated tour of the first nursing home candidate on your list.

Chapter 6
The Tour

This chapter takes you on a tour of a nursing home and introduces you to all pertinent staff members. You will learn the educational requirements and professional responsibilities of each position. Interview questions for each staff member are listed followed by a discussion of appropriate answers and misleading remarks. Fraudulent scams receive special attention.

Scheduling the Tour

With a working knowledge of Medicare regulations, you are ready to take an informed tour of each nursing home candidate. Actually, you will take two tours: The first is a scheduled tour with the administrator, director of nurses, or other **tour guide** designated by the facility.

The second is an unscheduled tour. It is very short and will serve to verify that your observations of the scheduled tour were the actual operation of the building rather than a choreographed show designed to impress prospective customers.

Your tour may be conducted by the admissions coordinator or someone from the marketing department, instead of the facility administrator. This is especially common in corporate-owned facilities. If your visit is scheduled with someone other than the administrator or director of nurses, make a note to request to meet each of these two individuals at some point during the tour.

It is the responsibility of the administrator to operate the nursing home, while the director of nurses is responsible for the medical care of the residents.

Building Approach

Your observations actually begin long before you enter the front door of the nursing home. As you approach the building, consider the following. Is it easily accessible? Are the grounds well kept? If the exterior is well-groomed, the interior will probably be sleek as well. The reason for this is that if costs need to be cut, the maintenance and grounds-keeping staff are cut first.

Is there enough parking for visitors? If there is not enough parking for visitors, they probably **do not get many visitors**.

As you enter the building, stop just inside the front door. Take a deep breath. What do you smell? Is there an odor? If you smell any noxious odors, such as urine, ammonia or a strong cleaner, this building is not clean.

Look around. Are there any residents near you? How do they look? Are they clean? Do they look well cared for? Do they look happy? Are they tied to their wheelchairs?

Scan the walls near the entrance to the building. Posted conspicuously near the front entrance, you should find the administrator's license and the nursing home license authorizing their operation within the state. Read them closely. Are they current? Make a note of the name on the administrator's license for verification that this is the person who is operating this nursing home. It is a common practice for the license on the wall to **belong to the regional manager of the corporation** while the individual running the facility is a student in training to be an administrator. This situation is legal so long as the student is adequately supervised. In reality, the supervision is minimal and on an infrequent basis since the regional manager is seldom on the premises.

After you have been in the building for a few minutes, you will be approached by a staff member. Expect to be greeted. If you are not greeted by a staff member within a few minutes of entering the building there is a security problem. Members of the public should never be allowed to wander into a nursing home, loiter around an entrance or exit, or wander around the building. This building is home to these residents. Just as you would not allow strangers to wander around your home, they should not be allowed to wander around a nursing home.

If a stranger is allowed to wander into the building, a resident could wander away from the nursing home. A confused resident will walk away with no regard for their own personal safety or their state of dress. This is a frequent story on the evening newscast. If this nursing home lacks adequate security, mark them off your list and leave.

After you have been greeted by a staff member and have been introduced to your tour guide, request that a copy of their most recent state survey report be available for your review before you leave the nursing home. They are required by law to have this document available to the public, so do not hesitate to ask for it. This document is the nursing homes report card and includes a list of citations which the nursing home received from the state investigators on their last survey.

The survey report will specify how many of those citations are categorized as Level A which indicate a potential life-threatening situation.

If the survey report reflects a poor survey, the nursing home administrator may attempt to prevent you from reviewing it. To that end, he may state that it has been misplaced, that it is not for public scrutiny, or that they don't have one. Each of these excuses is a blatant lie! Every nursing home is presented with a written survey report after every state survey. The law requires this report to be readily available for public review at all times. Therefore, if you are prevented from reviewing this document for any reason, cancel your tour and leave. Mark this candidate off your list and move on to the next one.

Tour Guide

This individual may be the administrator, director of nurses or other staff member. In a corporate owned nursing home, a member of the marketing department may be assigned this duty.

Responsibilities

Regardless of the identity of this person, their responsibility as tour guide is to show the nursing home in its most favorable light. You are a potential customer so, like any salesperson, they are trying to sell you something: The services of their nursing home.

In their attempt to achieve this goal, they will emphasize the attributes of this nursing home which set them apart from all others. You will be shown their best areas and diverted away from their problem areas.

Included in every tour should be the nurses station, dining room, physical therapy department, and a resident's bedroom. A highlight of the tour is the Medicare wing since this section has the best equipment and receives the majority of the staff's attention. You can expect to be steered away from the Medicaid wing of the building since this section receives substandard equipment and little staff attention.

This discrepancy between the care provided in Medicare and Medicaid sections is a result of the different reimbursement rates of these two programs with Medicare sporting a high rate and Medicaid suffering from a low one.

Your tour guide will do their best to avoid the wing which houses the wandering residents and those residents with mental disabilities. These residents lack social graces and are frequently ignored by the staff. These residents yell for no apparent reason, strike out at passersby, and drool. Some of them are desperate for physical contact and hug or kiss anyone within reach. Others will mistake you for someone from their past and greet you according to that past relationship. Profanity and sexually explicit language is also common.

You need to know if any residents of this nursing home are suffering from these conditions. To avoid any misconceptions regarding this nursing home, ask to tour the entire building, not just those areas considered marketable.

Interview Questions

Listed below are some general questions which should be asked of the tour guide. Regardless of their background, your tour guide should be able to answer these simple questions:

1. How many residents live in this nursing home?
2. How many beds are in this nursing home?
3. How many employees are on staff?
4. How many staff members take care of the residents?

    5. How many of your residents are on Medicare today?

    6. How many Medicare certified beds are in this nursing home?

    7. How many patients were discharged back to their homes, outside of the facility last month?

    8. When does discharge planning begin?

    9. How long have you worked here?

  10. Is there a licensed physical therapist on staff?

The answers to these ten questions will provide basic information regarding the daily operation of this nursing home:

1. How many residents live in the nursing home?
2. How many beds are in the nursing home?

These two questions will inform you as to the total capacity of the nursing home and the current census. A low census raises the question: Why is the census so low? The most common reason for a low census is a poor survey resulting in **stop placement** status. For example, Liberty Hills Nursing Home was cited for numerous Level A violations on their state survey which was completed last week. As a result of these citations, the survey team put them on stop placement status. This term means that Liberty Hills Nursing Home is prohibited from admitting any new residents until these violations are corrected. Therefore, if any residents are discharged or die during this time, those resulting vacancies cannot be filled. When these issues are resolved, the survey team returns for a re-examination. If they are satisfied, the survey team re-instates Liberty Hills' admission status. If you toured Liberty Hills

Nursing Home just after their admission status was restored, their census would still be low.

From these two questions you will also learn if there are any beds available at this time. If there are no beds available, and if there is a waiting list, it is doubtful that a vacancy will occur before your deadline.

3. **How many employees are on staff?**
4. **How many staff members take care of the residents?**

There are some employees such as maintenance and housekeeping, have little contact with the residents, but they are necessary to ensure a safe and clean living environment for the residents.

Question number four concerns our primary focus, care giving staff members. The answer to this question should be a high number, approximating the number of total employees. If this is not the case, the administrator is wasting his staff on other pursuits instead of caring for the residents.

Questions one and four, reveal the **ratio of residents to care-giving staff**. It is vital to have a low resident to care-giver ratio in order to provide adequate care. If there is a high number of residents per care-giver, this nursing home cannot provide adequate care; they simply do not have enough staff assigned to care for their residents.

This is similar to the situation of parents searching for a school for their child. The student-teacher ratio is a prominent consideration. If there are too many students, the teacher is unable to give adequate attention to each one. This is the same in the nursing home. If there are too many residents, the care-giver cannot take care of them all.

   5. How many of your residents are on Medicare today?
   6. How many Medicare certified beds are in the nursing home?

These two questions will reveal the ratio of Medicare patients to Medicare-certified beds. Ideally, this ratio should be high. A high ratio means that these beds are occupied, indicating that this nursing home admits Medicare patients frequently. In order to admit Medicare Part A patients frequently, this nursing home must be familiar with the regulations and is successful in the Medicare system. By contrast, a low ratio means that many of these beds are vacant or that they are occupied with non-Medicare residents. Either way, this nursing home admitted few Medicare patients recently, or none at all. Their limited exposure to the Medicare admission process and regulations is a concern.

If there are no Medicare-certified beds in this nursing home, they are not enrolled in the Medicare program. If your loved one is admitted to this nursing home, Medicare will not pay for their care. End the tour, mark this nursing home off your list and move on.

   7. How many patients were discharged back to their homes, outside of the facility, last month?

The wording of this question must be precise to avoid distortion of the answer. Coastal Convalescent Center is a prime example. This building has an infirmary wing for those with acute illness, a residential wing for those who cannot live on their own, and independent apartments for those who need assistance solely with laundry and heavy chores.

While touring this nursing home, if you asked the question "How many people were discharged last month?", the answer you receive will include many groups of people none of whom actually left the building. The first group consists of those patients who were admitted from the hospital, then transferred from the infirmary wing to the residential wing because they were unable to return to their own homes. These patients were discharged from the infirmary but not from the building. The second group consists of members of the residential wing who were in the infirmary temporarily due illness. Their discharge from the infirmary back to their room in the residential wing will be included in the answer. The patient was discharged back home but their home is the residential wing of this building. The third group consists of patients who have died. While this is not the intent of your question, technically **every resident who died was discharged**.

The point here is to be specific. If you ask the question, "How many people were discharged last month?", the response you receive will be misleading. Depending on the nursing home, the answer may include all discharges from the infirmary or "Medicare section" of the nursing home, as well as the residential sections **regardless of the destination of that patient**. By including all of these groups of "discharges" in their answer, your tour guide is able to give you the highest figure possible while appearing to tell the truth.

In order to obtain the information you are seeking, ask the very specific question, "How many patients were discharged back to their homes, outside of the nursing home, last month?"

8. When does discharge planning begin?

The answer to this question will indicate the progressive policies of this nursing home is in actively pursuing discharge as for every resident. **Discharge planning should begin as soon as the resident is admitted.** All goals and efforts of the staff, family, and the patient should be geared toward discharge if the following conditions are met. This patient must demonstrate reasonable potential for discharge back to society. The patient and family must favor discharge. The incredulous situation of the patient and family desiring permanent placement is a rare occurrence. This decision of the ultimate goal, belongs to the patient and his family to not the nursing home administration or staff.

Since the nursing home is reimbursed by the state on a per-patient basis, the financial incentive for the nursing home administration is to retain all patients who are admitted. This financial and ethical dilemma places the administration and patients in opposition. Most patients want to be rehabilitated so they can return home. However, the administrator receives higher payment if they stay permanently.

Nursing home administrators often need to be reminded that as a health care facility, the mission of the nursing home is to discharge all appropriate patients back to their homes in the community. A high success rate of discharging patients back to their homes also translates into higher profits for the nursing home through improved public relations and increased admissions. Although this is a simple concept, nursing home administrators seem to be unable to see past that initial drop in census as residents return home.

Higher profits should be considered a goal by the entire staff of any business operation. Amazingly, this is not the case in the nursing home industry if it means a change from the status quo. Even when this improved public image results in increased admissions, the administrator, office staff, and nursing staff complain about the increased paperwork. They prefer to admit patients for the remainder of their lives. If this attitude is prevalent in this nursing home, strike it from your list and move on.

9. How long have you worked here?

This question should be asked of every staff member you meet in the nursing home. The answers reveal the rate of staff turn-over. A low rate of turn-over reflects happy employees, resulting in better care for the residents. If there is a high rate of staff turn-over, delete this candidate from your list.

10. Is there a licensed physical therapist on staff?

The answer to this question should definetly be a clear "yes". A physical therapist must be available to residents requiring physical therapy services, but these may be provided by a **contractor** rather than an employee. State and federal regulations mandate that rehabilitation services must be provided or obtained for those residents who require it. Even if there is no PT employed by the nursing home, one must be available. Inform your tour guide that you wish to speak to the physical therapist.

Therapy Department

In response to this request, your tour guide should take you to the therapy room. If your tour guide replies that they do not have a therapy department, end your tour, mark this facility off your list and proceed to the next one.

As you step into the PT department, look around. The condition of the physical therapy equipment will indicate the quality of rehabilitation services provided. Does the equipment appear clean and in good working order? The equipment which should be present in every nursing home therapy department is as follows:

- Raised padded mat table
- Adjustable parallel bars
- Overhead pulley system
- Standing table

A raised, padded mat table is a padded mat, such as an exercise mat, on a raised platform. This raised mat is used for a variety of exercises. The platform should be approximately 16 to 18 inches high, which is the height of a standard wheelchair. Having the raised mat the same height as the residents wheelchair helps to ensure a safe **transfer** from the wheelchair to the mat.

Adjustable parallel bars are two parallel bars which are adjustable in height and width, mounted on a wooden platform. They are used to re-train residents in the skills of standing, walking, and balance. An over-the-head pulley system is a system of pulleys and two ropes, one for each hand. This apparatus hangs overhead, so it can be used in a seated position to stretch the shoulders and arms. A standing table consists of a table top, mounted on a standing frame, with safety straps, and padding to secure the resident in a standing position.

It is vital that all of this equipment is serviceable and in good repair. It is common for the administrator to attempt to cut costs in this area. For example, at Pine Meadows Care Center, the administrator provided the therapy department with a set of parallel bars constructed by a maintenance man from old, leaded plumbing pipe. This pipe had been removed from the nursing home's plumbing system due to the risk of lead exposure to the residents. Removing these pipes from the water supply system of the building eliminated the risk of lead exposure through the drinking water. However, using them as makeshift parallel bars put the residents at risk for lead exposure through touch. In an effort to cut costs, the nursing home traded one potential health risk for another.

Ask to see the license of the physical therapist and any PTA working in this nursing home. These licenses should be hanging on the wall of the physical therapy department in a conspicuous location. Verify that the license hanging on the wall belongs to the PT or PT assistant working in that nursing home. These licenses should be issued from the state in which the nursing home is located. This information is printed conspicuously on the front of each license.

Physical Therapist

This individual is a rehabilitation professional whose goal is to improve the strength and mobility of the residents. To achieve this goal, the PT utilizes a wide variety of training and exercises which they have learned over many years of academic and clinical study.

Education

All physical therapists have completed a minimum of four years of college education, graduated with at least a Bachelor's of Science Degree in Physical Therapy, and passed a licensure examination for the state in which they practice. This license must be renewed annually. In order to be granted re-licensure, the PT must complete continuing education courses to further advance their skills.

Responsibilities

The attention of physical therapist is directed primarily at the newly admitted resident. The therapist must provide services to all of these residents who require them and to administer the Medicare Part A physical therapy benefits to all residents who qualify. Since the ultimate goal for many residents is to return to their own homes, this goal should be shared by the PT and the entire staff if there is reasonable potential. For example, Mrs. Taylor is 92 years old and suffered a massive stroke. She is unable to use her arms or legs and has no feeling in them, at all. Her chances of returning to her own home is virtually nonexistent and to encourage her in this hope would be unethical. Another new admission, Mr. Emery is 68 years old and suffered a broken hip when he fell in the bathroom. His hip was surgically repaired in the hospital and his chances of returning home are very good.

The physical therapist has a secondary responsibility to the current residents, who have lived in the nursing home for a longer period of time. That responsibility is to provide physical therapy services to all of these residents who require them and to administer the Medicare Part B physical therapy benefits to all those who qualify. This requires the PT to screen all residents who may have had a recent change in their abilities whether that change is for the better or worse. The goal here is to assist the resident to become as independent as possible for the remainder of their lives and to improve the quality of that resident's life. For example, Mrs. Alder is an 87 year old, long-term resident of the nursing home who has pushed herself around in a wheelchair for years. Recently, her stooped posture has become so bad that she can no longer look up to see where she is going. She frequently runs into furniture or walls and is at risk for injury. This resident should be seen by the PT for an adapted seating system to improve her sitting posture in her wheelchair allowing her to sit more upright. She could then continue to push herself around the nursing home thus preserving some of her independence.

Another responsibility of the physical therapist is to the nursing home staff. As an expert in the areas of physical mobility, muscle strength and coordination, and adaptive equipment, the PT is charged with the task of educating others. This education takes many forms. The PT must educate the certified nurse's aides in proper lifting techniques to prevent back injuries on the job. The PT must educate the entire nursing staff in proper positioning of the residents in bed and in a wheelchair to ensure comfort and prevent **contractures**. The PT must train the CNAs in proper exercises to prevent these contractures. The PT must train the RNA in the maintenance program designed specifically for a particular resident. The PT must educate the licensed nurses in the indications for therapy intervention. The licensed nurse must be able to identify residents as possible rehab candidates since they are in the building 24 hours per day and the PT is present only two or three hours five days per week.

Scams

The progressive physical therapist accepts and fulfills these responsibilities admirably. Just as every profession has its bad eggs, physical therapy is no exception and the nursing home industry seems to attract more than its share. Instead of assisting the residents and educating the staff, some PTs are there to collect a paycheck for the bare minimum of work. They spend most of their time in meetings in which nothing is accomplished and attending social activities with the residents. While participating in these social functions is pleasant, that is the job of the Social Activities Department not the Physical Therapy Department. In shirking their responsi-bilities these PTs are actually on-the-job retired.

On occasion, a skilled and ethical therapist gets caught up in the web of nursing home scams. This occurs when she is coerced by the administrator to discharge a resident from therapy services as soon as their money runs out. This violates federal and state laws, Medicare guidelines, and Medicaid regulations, but it is a common occurrence. For example, Mrs. Smith has been treated by the PT under Medicare Part A coverage. Her allotted 100 days of coverage runs out tomorrow and Medicare will no longer pay for her therapy. The nursing home administrator informs the PT that she must discharge the patient tomorrow. The therapist objects stating that physical therapy treatment programs must be based on the needs of the patient not on financial bias. The administrator then threatens the therapist with loss of her job if she refuses to follow his direction. This places the therapist in a difficult position. If she discharges Mrs. Smith, she is violating federal and state laws. If she doesn't, she loses her job. By issuing this threat the administrator has already violated the law, however this misconduct is rarely reported to the proper authorities.

Therapy Support
The staff of some nursing homes includes a PTA as well as a PT. Pay close attention when this occurs. Physical therapy assistants are not licensed in all states so there is little or no regulation of this individual. Even the minimal regulation which may be present in your state, is not consistent in all states. In some states, a PTA is a graduate from a two year physical therapy assistant program, is licensed by the state in which they practice, and completes continuing education courses to qualify for annual license renewal. The laws of these states clearly mandate the procedures which a PTA is qualified to perform. In these states, there is no gray area concerning what a PTA can and cannot do on the job.

By contrast, other states may offer a two year physical therapy assistant program which a PTA should attend. However, there are no laws mandating this educational requirement. In addition, there is no licensure of PTAs, so there is no way to enforce an education requirement.

As a result of inadequate regulation of physical therapy assistants as a profession, many of them perform whatever activities they choose regardless of their lack of proper training. The **malpractice** and the risk of injury to the resident is completely disregarded since there is no professional or legal accountability.

While not all PTAs practice in this ruthless manner, there are many who do. Until there is adequate regulation of these individuals, let the resident beware.

Interview Questions

While talking to the PT, there are a number of questions which you need to ask. All of the information necessary to answer these questions should be readily available in the physical therapy department:

1. How many patients are receiving physical therapy services under Medicare Part A insurance coverage?
2. How many patients are receiving physical therapy services under Medicare Part B insurance coverage?
3. How many patients are receiving physical therapy services under private insurance coverage?
4. How many patients are receiving physical therapy services under Medicaid?
5. Are you involved with the Restorative Nursing Care program?
6. If the answer to 5 is "Yes", what is your involvement with the Restorative Nursing Care program?
7. Do you perform **home evaluations**?
8. How long have you worked here?
9. Are you an employee or a contractor?
10. How many hours per day do you work here?
11. Do you work in this nursing home every day?

The answers to these questions will give you a basic understanding of how the physical therapy department operates. You will also obtain a good indication of how the physical therapy department interacts with other staff members.

1. **How many patients are receiving physical therapy services under Medicare Part A insurance coverage?**
2. **How many patients are receiving physical therapy services under Medicare Part B insurance coverage?**
3. **How many patients are receiving physical therapy services under private insurance coverage?**
4. **How many patients are receiving physical therapy services under Medicaid?**

This series of questions will reveal the attitude of the administration regarding their physical therapy services. Residents should be treated according to their need for services with finances as a secondary consideration. Too often these services are rationed only to those residents who are most able to pay. A resident's PT program may even be discontinued completely when their Medicare Part A coverage begins to wane at day 21 regardless of the resident's need for therapy. If therapy services continue after day 21, they most certainly will be discontinued by day 101 at which time Medicare stops paying the bill.

5. **Are you involved with the Restorative Nursing Care Program?**

If the answer is no, then the Restorative Nursing Care Program is not up to optimal standards. If "yes", continue with the next question.

6. **What is your involvement with the Restorative Nursing Care Program?**

These two questions will reveal information regarding the Restorative Nursing Care Program and how it functions. Some nursing homes take pride in the excellent quality of their Restorative Nursing Care Program and the benefits which this program brings to the residents in the form of improved functional abilities. However, the majority of nursing homes have only a shadow of what a Restorative Nursing Care Program should be. Due to the minimum requirements of the regulations of most states, this substandard program may be compliant. Even a substandard program may satisfy the regulations which simply state that the nursing home must have one. There is no required standard by which this program must function.

The appropriate answer to these questions five and six is that she evaluates each of the patients and designs an appropriate restorative program, with training of all appropriate staff members. The PT should also monitor the programs periodically and make any necessary adjustments.

7. Do you perform home evaluations?

This question is vital to your loved one's chances of returning to their home, outside of the nursing home. The definition of a **home evaluation** is an examination of the resident's home if discharge outside of the nursing home is anticipated. Just prior to discharge, the PT, OT, and the resident should visit the home to which the resident will be discharged. This could be the resident's own home or the home of a family member. The PT will evaluate the resident's abilities to move around the house and go up and down stairs. The OT will evaluate the resident's abilities to get into and out of the bathtub or shower, prepare meals, and any other activities in the resident's daily home life.

Other areas addressed by these therapists are the resident's ability to access the telephone in case of an emergency, the possibility of meals on wheels, laundry services and housecleaning. The therapists will make recommendations for adaptive equipment needed by the resident to make the transition back home easier and more successful. This adaptive equipment might include a bath bench or hand-held shower which can be installed prior to the patient's homecoming. If any structural changes are needed, such as a ramp, this can also be completed prior to discharge. In this way, the resident, their family, and their home are all prepared for this resident's return home and there is a good chance they will be able to remain home for a long time to come. A thorough home evaluation is vital to a successful discharge.

8. How long have you worked here?

She is the second staff member to answer this question. Asking this question of the nursing home staff will reveal the rate of staff turn-over.

A physical therapist will, typically work in a nursing home as an employee for two to four years. The primary reason for a therapist to leave the employment of a nursing home is coercion by the administrator to discharge a resident from rehab before they are ready. Of equal importance is the insistence by the administrator to use substandard equipment putting the resident and the therapist at risk for injury.

Coercion from the administrator is not limited to discharging residents from rehab prematurely. It is common for the administrator to attempt to persuade the therapist to document the work of the RNAs as skilled physical therapy. If the administrator is successful in his persuasion, s/he can deceptively bill Medicare for these services as if the PT provided them. The PT is responsible for this fraudulent billing since she completes the logs. This is another instance in which the therapist must choose between her job and the law. It is unfortunate for the therapist that this coercion is difficult to prove since it is the therapist's word against the administrator's. If the therapist chooses to uphold the law and try to keep her job, she has the option of reporting this incident to the corporate owners. However, without hard evidence she will be hard pressed to convince them. Being the higher ranking employee, the administrator is believed and the therapist is asked to resign.

On rare occasions, a PT will choose to leave the employment of a nursing home due to professional conflicts with the nursing staff. However, conflicts with the nursing staff are commonplace and should not result in the loss of a good therapist.

9. Are you an employee or a contractor?
10. How many hours per day do you work here?
11. Do you work in this nursing home every day?

These three questions will reveal the working relationship between the physical therapist and the nursing home administrator.

If this therapist is an employee, the chances are great that your relative will have the same PT every day. However, employee status does not guarantee that the therapist works solely in this nursing home. Although the therapist is a full time employee, they may not spend the whole day at this nursing home. It is a common practice for an administrator to hire a therapist and contract her services out to another nursing home part-time. In effect, one therapist is shared by more than one nursing home. This arrangement is acceptable when the caseload in both nursing homes is light. However, what happens when the caseload of both buildings fluctuates beyond what a part-time therapist can manage. One therapist cannot provide therapy services for the residents of both buildings when the caseload of both buildings is high. Some residents receive shortened treatments while others will receive no treatments at all.

If the therapist is a contractor employed by a large therapy contracting company, s/he will work in more than one nursing home on any given day, and will work at this particular nursing home for only two or three hours per day. Other therapists from the same company will be assigned to the same building, so a patient may have a different therapist every day. In this situation, **continuity of care** is a serious concern, especially if your loved one suffers from confusion or dementia. The term continuity of care refers to the resident receiving the same or similar treatment every day from the same therapist. This regularity drastically improves the progress achieved by the resident and speeds up the time required to achieve that progress. In essence, the resident gets better faster and achieves greater overall independence. This is especially important to the resident who suffers from confusion or dementia since they have difficulty following instructions and remembering the treatment from the day before.

The personal relationship between the resident and therapist greatly enhances the resident's progress.

Obviously, this relationship cannot grow if the resident is treated by a different therapist everyday.

Restorative Nursing Aide

The staff of each nursing home should include several Restorative Nursing Aides (RNA) whom can be found at the therapy department.

Education

This individual should be certified as a CNA by completing a seven week course in general care techniques and passing a certification exam. CNA certification should be followed by a course in restorative nursing techniques and on-the-job training from the PT, OT, and SLP, but this is not a job requirement or a certification requirement. It is not mandatory that an RNA be certified as a CNA in preparation for the position. There are no regulations governing the education of the RNA, so they may or may not be adequately trained. Since training costs money and administrators do not like to spend money, RNAs seldom receive proper training.

Responsibilities

This poorly trained staff member is responsible for administering the maintenance programs designed specifically for a particular resident. Ideally, these maintenance programs are designed by the PT, OT, and the SLP. After being trained in the particulars of each patient-specific maintenance program, both the patient and the program are turned over to the RNA. From that time onward the maintenance program is carried out by the aide with periodic monitoring by the therapist. Therefore, this employee plays a key role in the functional status of each resident, and in their chances of retaining their abilities to walk, dress, and eat without assistance.

Scams

There are many unethical and illegal scams involving the RNA, most of which utilize manipulation or threats.

If there is a temporary increase in the restorative nursing caseload, the administrator will require the RNAs to work overtime rather shift his personnel or hire another staff member.

A common reaction of the administrator to a high restorative caseload is to require the RNAs to provide these treatments without authorizing their overtime. Therefore, if they do work overtime they do not get paid for it. This violates state law but is rarely reported due to the RNAs' fear of losing their jobs.

A heavy caseload will also result when the administrator down-sizes the staff in an effort to cut operating costs. In this instance, both the RNAs and the residents suffer but the suffering of the residents is compounded when this overworked employee resigns.

Coercion from the administrator to perform procedures beyond their skill level is illegal but occurs with shocking regularity. If the RNA refuses, she is fired. If she submits to this pressure, she is breaking the law, in addition to putting herself and the resident at risk for an injury. If she reports this coercion to the corporate owners, the administrator will deny it. Being the higher ranking employee, the corporate owners will believe the administrator and again, the RNA is fired.

Employees should report it to the state authorities, but since there is no state licensure or regulations governing the practice of RNAs, they frequently are unaware of their responsibilities as health professionals.

The last option to the RNA is to confide in her supervising nurse whom is either a rehabilitation nurse or a charge nurse. Although required by state law to report these incidents, the nurse will ignore the transgression to avoid getting involved. Consequently, these incidents of misconduct are rarely reported.

Administrative coercion also takes a complimentary tone. The suave administrator is able to phrase his directions in such a way that the RNA feels flattered. The administrator convinces the RNA that she is sufficiently skilled to perform these treatments so she never suspects the truth. In this way, the administrator accomplishes his goal of having a lesser skilled and lower paid employee do the work. The RNA feels complimented with no suspicion of the risks to herself or the resident.

The chances of this incident of professional misconduct be reported are minimal since the RNA is unaware that one occurred. However if by chance it is reported, the administrator denies the incident and denies any knowledge of the RNA practicing beyond her skill level. The administrator will receive only a minimal reprimand or none at all but the RNA loses her job and is barred from working with the elderly in the future.

Interview Questions

While there are several RNAs on staff, an interview with one of them will suffice. Listed below are the questions for the RNA:

1. How long have you worked here?
2. What training have you had in order to perform this job?

3. How many hours per day do you work?
4. How many residents are you scheduled to work with, today?

The answers to the preceding questions will indicate the training and workload of the RNAs. This, in turn, will reflect the quality of care received by the residents.

1. How long have you worked here?

When the answer to this question is combined with the answers from other staff members to this same question, you will obtain an accurate indication of the rate of staff turn-over in this nursing home.
Typically, a RNA will remain in the employ of a nursing home for several years. They begin their employment as a CNA and are later promoted to the position of RNA. However, since there are no standard education or training requirements for the RNA position, they do not have to possess CNA certification. They could be any individual who applied for a job and lacking all appropriate education and skills.

2. What training have you had in order to perform the duties of this job?

As mentioned in the RNA education section of this chapter, in some nursing homes an applicant for this position must first be certified as a nurses' aide and have the medical title of Certified Nurses' Aid. That includes a high school diploma or equivalent, a seven week course in nurses' aide training and pass a written certification examination. With this certification, they acquire the title of Certified Nurses' Aide (CNA). They are then qualified to provide general care for nursing home residents and apply for this position. However, since no regulations exist governing the practice of restorative nursing, the enforcement of these requirements is left to the discretion of the individual nursing home. One nursing home may choose to enforce these regulations while another may choose to ignore them. With   this lack of regulation, anyone could walk into a nursing home and be hired as an RNA. If a nursing home is short-staffed and needs someone to fill the position that RNA, the administrator will hire any applicant regardless of their qualifications or lack of them.

Ideally, an RNA has attended an eight week training course in Restorative Nursing Techniques. Unfortunately, in most nursing homes this training is ignored, so they have no formal training to qualify them to perform the duties of restorative nursing. In addition, each RNA should receive on-the-job training from the PT, OT, and SLP which includes the general principals of rehabilitation and the maintenance programs of the specific residents whom will be assigned to their caseload. However, since this training costs money and the administrator is hesitant to spend any money, this on-the-job training is seldom completed. Therefore, the RNA receives no training to perform the duties of her job description.

A specific concern involves the **patient-specific** maintenance programs. Does the RNA receive training from the therapist who designed this program, prior to administering it? The therapist is responsible for documenting the content of the training and the staff members whom were trained. In most nursing homes, this training does not take place so the resident's medical chart lacks this required documentation. A more serious concern arises when the therapist is not involved in the design of the maintenance program at all. This is a common situation in which the RNA is directed by the administrator to design the maintenance program herself.

Designing a **resident-specific** maintenance program requires a thorough evaluation of their functional abilities, the specific living situation, adaptive equipment needs and their goals for how independent they want to be. The therapist must consider all of these areas and design an exercise program which will maintain their highest level of functioning with their desired amount of independence.

The following example illustrates this point. Mr. Bates is a long term resident of the Peaceful Meadows Convalescent Home. He uses a wheelchair to get around and has no interest in regaining his walking abilities. He was able to move by himself from his bed to his wheelchair and back again, and from his wheelchair to the toilet and back again. He was very happy with this level of functioning and independence until he suffered a mild case of the flu which weakened his condition. He now requires assistance for those bed and toilet transfers and he is offended by this lack of privacy. He wants his independence back.

In this example, Mr. Bates requires a physical and functional evaluation by the therapist. His needs include a strengthening exercise program, retraining in bed transfers, wheelchair transfers, and toilet transfers. All of these tasks require the skills of a physical therapist. A licensed physical therapist will design a maintenance program to address all of these areas so Mr. Bates goal of independent transfers will be realized. The therapist will then train the RNAs in the specific program and document all of this in Mr. Bates medical chart.

   3. **How many hours per day do you work?**
   4. **How many residents are you scheduled to work with today?**

The answers to these two questions will inform you of the working conditions in this nursing home. They will indicate if the nursing home is understaffed, as they frequently are.

Question number three will reveal if the RNA is overworked, on a regular basis. If the restorative nursing department is understaffed, each RNA is required to work longer hours without pay or treat a heavier resident caseload during the same work day. The resulting physical and mental fatigue will result in a lower quality of care for the residents and risk for injury to the RNA and the resident. Overworked employees make mistakes. One example is the RNA who forgets to lock the brakes of the wheelchair before assisting the resident to stand up. The wheelchair slides out from under the resident before they are safely on their feet, depositing them abruptly on the floor.

The answer to question number four, "How many residents are you scheduled to work with, today?" will reveal the amount of work each RNA is required to complete in one day. In some nursing homes each RNA is scheduled to work with as many as 30 residents in one day. If each maintenance program could be completed in as little as 20 minutes, it would still take 10 hours to treat 30 residents. The standard workday of the RNA is 8 hours and the administrator seldom authorizes overtime to treat their assigned 30 residents. Therefore, the RNA provides substandard treatments in order to stay within the standard 8 hour work day or she works for free. This reoccurring dilemma results in a frustrated, overworked employee, as well as a lower quality of care for the residents. There is also a significant risk for injury to each resident during their maintenance exercise program which is performed too quickly by an over-worked, poorly-trained RNA.

Charge Nurse

This professional is responsible for the medical care of each resident in her section of the building and supervises all other nurses and nurses' aides assigned to her section.

Education

In order to comply with federal and state regulations, the charge nurse in a nursing home must be a licensed practical nurse (LPN) or a registered nurse (RN). This sounds like a straightforward mandate, but it is not that simple.

Since the nursing profession is governed by the laws of each state and those laws vary, the nurses of one state practice under different laws than nurses in neighboring states. This is the basis for much confusion. Some states are very specific in mandating the educational require-ments, qualifications, and duties of each level of the nursing profession including nurses' aid, LPN, RN, **BSN**, and **Nurse Practitioner**. However, many other states are not.

In one state these levels are very distinct. A nurses' aide requires one year of training, an LPN requires two years of formal education, an RN requires three years, a **Bachelor of Science degree in Nursing** or BSN requires four years, and a nurse practitioner is a post-graduate degree. Other states are not so specific. A nurses' aide or CNA requires only seven weeks of training, an LPN requires one to two years of training and an RN should have two to three years of training, but the specific amount of training for each of these levels is not defined. Only the BSN and nurse practitioner have specific educational requirements since they include college degrees. This identity crisis among the nursing staff of the nursing home industry requires the consumer to question the charge nurse about her credentials.

In addition to entry level training, continuing education raises concern. The laws of some states mandate that all RNs and LPNs take continuing education courses to maintain their state licensure. However, a few states ignore this issue.

Continuing education is not a requirement for employment in the nursing home industry. In fact, many administrators openly discourage training of any kind since these courses require time off from work. This discourage takes many forms, just one of which is refusing to assist employees with enrollment expenses. Consequently, many nurses in the nursing home industry forego all continuing education and their skills decline.

Responsibilities

The responsibilities of the charge nurse encompass the care of all residents in their section of the building and supervision of lower ranking nurses and nurses' aides caring for them. They must perform an examination on any resident suffering an illness or change in their condition and document their findings in the resident's medical chart. This information must be communicated to the resident's physician and any new orders for treatment or medication changes must be implemented including consultations with other health professionals. Finally, the charge nurse must contact the resident's family with news of this change and of all professional consultations.

Although each of these tasks is the responsibility of the charge nurse, she frequently fails to complete them. This was illustrated in the example of Mrs. Smith, who had fallen. In this case it was the responsibility of the charge nurse to examine Mrs. Smith for injuries and take the appropriate actions listed below:

1. The physician should be informed of this change in her condition.
2. The PT should be consulted for the possibility of treating Mrs. Smith.
3. Her family should be notified of her fall.
4. Her family should be informed of the steps taken to prevent additional falls.
5. The incident and follow-up should be completely documented.

All of these consultations should have been documented in the medical chart. Instead of completing these required duties, this charge nurse directed the RNA to put a walker in Mrs. Smith's room.

Scams

The failure of the charge nurse to fulfill her duties has many causes, one of which is the lack of continuing education. Since continuing education is not required by state law and nursing home administrators discourage it as increasing their operating costs, many nurses simply neglect to update their training. This lack of current knowledge leads to substandard resident examinations and lack of awareness for the need for rehab intervention.

The charge nurse fails to fulfill all of their responsibilities toward the residents if an incident occurs at the end of their shift. In many nursing homes, the administrator refuses to authorize any overtime so if a charge nurse works overtime, they do not get paid for it. Consequently, if a resident falls at the end of the shift, the charge nurse will ignore the incident, or leave it for the charge nurse coming on duty, rather than work overtime for free. For example, if Mrs. Smith fell at 2:30 PM and shift change is at 3:00 PM, the charge nurse will ignore it. If she fulfills her responsibility of examining Mrs. Smith, consulting the physician, consulting the therapist, informing the family, and documenting all of this information in Mrs. Smith's medical chart, she will work overtime.

As mentioned previously, the federal and state regulations mandate that an RN must be charge nurse on the day shift 7 days per week and an RN or LPN must be charge nurse during each shift. There are many ways used by administrators to avoid staffing the more expensive RN as charge nurse. One method is to title the 7:00 AM to 3:00 PM shift as the "day shift" and schedule an RN for that shift only. This leaves the Director of Nurses, whom by law must be at least an RN and usually works the standard 8:00 AM to 4:30 PM workday, to satisfy the RN requirement for the remainder of the day. Since the Director of Nurses goes home at 4:30 PM, there may only an LPN to fulfill all the responsibilities of the charge nurse position after that time. Therefore, if a resident falls or becomes ill between 7:00 AM and 4:30 PM, they will receive better care from nurses with more training than if they fall or become ill from 4:30 PM to 7:00 AM.

Interview Questions

The charge nurse is obviously an important staff member in any nursing home. Ask to speak with the charge nurse on duty in the section of the nursing home in which your relative would reside. The charge nurse should be able to answer the following questions:

1. How long have you worked here?
2. How many years of nursing school did you attend?
3. What was the topic of your most recent continuing education class and when was it held?
4. How often are the residents bathed? Can they be bathed more often if they wish?
5. At what times do the residents eat their meals?
6. How many residents in this nursing home are physically restrained?
7. How many residents in this nursing home are able to walk?
8. How many residents in this nursing home are in wheelchairs?
9. How many residents in this nursing home are bedbound?

The answers to the preceding questions will indicate the quality of care received by the residents in this section of the facility.

1. How long have you worked here?

As a key player in the successful operation of any nursing home, her answer is a contributing factor in this building's staff turnover rate, and her longevity indicates the staff dynamics in throughout the nursing department. The following example illustrates this.

At Golden Acres Retirement Home, the CNAs spend the majority of their time chatting among themselves and taking numerous breaks rather than caring for the residents. A recently hired charge nurse directs them back to their duties. They ignore her and continue their conversation. The charge nurse then consults with her supervisor, the Director of Nurses regarding this issue. The Director of Nurses cautions this new employee against upsetting any of the CNAs since they are difficult to replace if they choose to quit. Although the charge nurse is held responsible for the care of the residents, she is powerless in her role of supervisor without the support of the Director of Nurses. The result is a frustrated charge nurse, lazy CNAs, and poor care for the residents.

In the above situation, the ethical and professional charge nurse will report the situation to the authorities and resign. However, when faced with a situation of this nature, she rarely fulfills her ethical obligation. Once hired, a charge nurse seldom leaves the employment of a nursing home since they gain seniority in wages and benefits based solely upon longevity not on position or skills. Therefore, if they leave, they lose all benefits and must start at the bottom of the pay scale at the next nursing home. This financial incentive to ignore the situation makes it extremely rare for a charge nurse to comply with professional ethics and the state law by reporting such occurrences. Most charge nurses ignore all incidents and remain long term employees.

2. How many years of nursing school did you attend?

The charge nurse will answer this question by stating that s/he is an RN(Registered Nurse) or LPN(Licensed Practical Nurse). While that answer is informative, it does not answer the question. You need to know the quantity of her formal training. As mentioned previously, state regulations governing the nursing professions vary widely in their definitions of CNA, LPN, and RN. The result is that an RN could have two, three, or four years of nursing school, depending upon the State in which s/he lives. As a consumer, you have no way of knowing if you are talking to a two-, three- or four-year registered nurse, unless you.

3. What was the topic of your most recent continuing education class and when was it held?

This question will be received with some surprise since few people ask it. The answer to this question will reveal if this charge nurse continues to improve her skills and if she is supported by the administrator in doing so. In many states, LPNs are not required to take continuing education classes so their skills suffer as do the residents in their care. Although RNs have this requirement nursing home administrators discourage them from taking continuing education courses since these courses necessitate time off from work. Several methods commonly used to discourage continuing education are listed below.

1. S/he is not paid for their time attending these courses.
2. S/he must pay the enrollment fees herself.
3. S/he is refused time off to attend courses.

These methods are very effective in discouraging the RN from attending continuing education classes. In order to do so, she must pay the enrollment fee herself and attend the class on her day off with no reimbursement of her time or money. Since enrollment fees are paid several months in advance and the RN receives her work schedule in two week increments, scheduling a continuing education course is a gamble and a financial loss for late cancelation.

4. How often are the residents bathed? Can they bathe more often, if they wish?

Regardless of the obvious need for basic personal hygiene, nursing homes residents are bathed only once a week. Moreover, if the **bath aide** is absent, the residents scheduled for a bath that day will be skipped. (The term "bath aid" refers to the certified nurses' aide who is designated to bath the residents.) In a few facilities a family member may request that their loved one is bathed more than once a week, but this is not an option in all nursing homes.

5. What time do the residents eat their meals?

In addition to asking this question, ask for a copy of today's menu. This will reveal precisely what was served today. Merely asking what kind of food the nursing home serves, is too vague.

If possible, stay for lunch and request to eat in the residents' dining room. Expect to pay a nominal fee for this opportunity to sample the culinary fare and witness the mealtime care of the residents. In fact, the residents will receive better service and care, as a result of your presence. The meals will be served in a more timely fashion, hot food will be served hot and cold food will be served cold. In addition, the CNAs who are assigned to assist the residents with their meal will be more patient and tolerant if a visitor is present. All of these changes in the care of the residents occur when a visitor is present to witness their actions.

6. How many residents in this nursing home are physically restrained?

This issue has widespread legal ramifications in the areas of personal safety and human rights. As you walk through the nursing home on your tour, look for physical restraints tying residents to their wheelchairs. Ideally, there should be none in use, but a restraint can be under very specific circumstances. When a restraint is deemed necessary for the safety of the resident there must be evidence in their medical chart of a consultations with the PT or OT and with the resident's family or legal representative, prior to the restraint being applied. Regardless of these criteria, in many nursing homes physical restraints are applied by the CNA or at the direction of the charge nurse, for their convenience only. For example, Mr. Willows is uncomfortable sitting in his wheelchair and frequently tries to stand up by himself. After assisting him back down for the fifth time in the past hour, the frustrated will use a restraint to tie him to his wheelchair.

Since s/he is responsible for the residents in her section, the charge nurse should be able to give you an accurate count of those residents who are physically restrained. If s/he does not know this information, s/he is neglectful of her residents, since s/he is responsible for knowing their functional status at all times. If s/he is unwilling to answer this question, s/he is concealing information in violation of federal and state regulations governing the use of physical restraints.

The answers to next three questions will reveal if this nursing home is oriented to the rehabilitation of their residents and to maintaining the abilities which their residents still possess. They will also indicate the level of success of the entire rehab services program, including skilled physical therapy, occupational therapy and speech therapy.

7. How many residents in this nursing home are able to walk without someone assisting them?

The precise wording of this question is important, in order to obtain an accurate answer. The phrase "...walk without someone assisting them...", will ensure that accuracy. The pertinent information to be obtained is the number of people who can walk under their own power, whether that includes a walker, crutches, canes, etc. If you ask "How many residents in this nursing home can walk?", you will receive a variety of answers depending upon how that charge nurse chooses to interpret your question. The charge nurse may construe this to mean anyone who can walk with an assistive device and/or with the assistance of a CNA. This could include anyone who:

- Walks under his own power, just as you or I.
- Walks under his own power with a cane, crutches or a walker.

al
- Does not use a device at all but requires a person-
    assistant to accompany him due to a mental or
    psychological condition.
- Uses a walking device and one or more personal
    assistants.
- Participates in a restorative nursing ambulation
    program, with one or more personal assistants
    and a walking device.

This answer could also include all residents treated by the PT in an attempt to re-learn how to stand up in the parallel bars. These residents have a long way to go before they can walk by themselves but they could be included in this answer if the charge nurse so choses. The answer you receive to the question, "How many residents in this nursing home can walk?", could include any number of the above-mentioned groups or all of them. Due to the broad range of interpretations, you must be specific in the wording of this question.

8. How many residents are in wheelchairs?

As previously, this one could be misinterpreted by the charge nurse to skew the information. Many residents who are able to walk by themselves with a cane or walker inside the facility, require a wheelchair for excursions out of the building. In addition, the number of residents using **posture-guard chairs** or **geri-chairs** should not be included in this answer. The answer to this question should include only those residents who use regular wheelchairs.

9. How many residents in this nursing home are bed bound?

State regulations require that all residents are turned in bed or shifted in their wheelchairs at least every two hours, either under their own power or by the staff. To comply with this regulation, the staff of some facilities will transfer a **bed-bound** resident to a posture-guard chair or geri-chair for a portion of the day. In this way, the resident can be moved out of the relative isolation of their room and can be moved easily about the nursing home for a change of scenery. Therefore, these residents are technically not bound to their beds all day because the nursing home staff is taking better than average care them.

In asking this question, the vital information is not the specific number of bed-bound residents but an indication of the care those residents receive. If the staff of the nursing home is getting these residents out of bed as they should, the number of bed-bound residents will be low.

Nurses' Aide

This individual provides direct care to the residents. S/he assists them with dressing, grooming, personal hygiene, pushing their wheelchair to meals, and any request they might make of her. Obviously, the proper education and training of this person is vital to the welfare of the residents.

Education

Federal and state regulations require that every personal care giver employed by a nursing home be certified as a nurses' aid. To receive this certification, an individual must complete a seven week training course in general nursing care techniques and pass an examination. At the time, the printed certification and the medical title of Certified Nurses' Aide is awarded.

The training of a CNA should be ongoing in the form of on-the-job courses provided by the rehab staff in assisting the resident in the following areas:

- Moving around in bed
- Getting in and out of bed
- Standing up from their wheelchair
- Proper positioning in bed and wheelchair
- Application of a physical restraint
- Use of a walker, cane, and crutches
- Feeding techniques
- Application of splints

The skills of the CNA should be enhanced on a regular basis with the latest information and techniques in each of these areas. However, since this training diverts staff members from their regular duties therefore costing money, the administrator discourages it.

Responsibilities

The CNA is responsible for the general daily care of the residents. Examples of this care includes the morning and nightly routines of washing, brushing their teeth, dressing, grooming and assistance in the bathroom. The CNA also transports the residents in their wheelchairs to meals and other activities in the nursing home.

Scams

In the general resident population, each CNA should be assigned approximately 7 residents on any given day and on the Medicare wing each CNA should be assigned a maximum of 4 residents. However, this is an ideal situation. It is more common for each CNA to be assigned 12 to 15 general care residents. On the Medicare wing which houses the acutely ill residents recently admitted from the hospital, each CNA is assigned 6 to 9 residents. The result is poor care for the residents.

The most blatant reason for inadequate resident care is neglect; the CNA simply ignore the pleas of the residents. Nothing is more distressing than the unanswered pleas of a resident needing to be taken to the bathroom. Clearly, this is negligence. The most common time of day for this to occur is near the end of a shift. Most nursing homes have three shifts: 7:00 AM to 3:00 PM, 3:00 PM to 11:00 PM, and 11:00 PM to 7:00 AM. As the work day for the CNA draws to an end, she leaves unpleasant duties for her replacement. Toileting a resident is considered the most unpleasant of all CNA duties and is most commonly neglected. If the resident was taken to the bathroom when they made their first request, there would be little or no mess to clean up. However, since the previous CNA neglected this resident, there will be a considerable and unpleasant mess for the next CNA coming on duty.

As you might expect, this situation creates conflict between the two CNAs which escalates rapidly and involves the using the residents as a means to inflict hardship. Of course, the resident is the one who suffers from these petty games.

Interview Questions
1. How long have you worked here?
2. What formal training qualifies you for this kind of work?
3. How many residents are in your care today?

The answers to the preceding questions will reveal the training and workload of the nurses' aide which in turn, will reflect the quality of care received by the residents.

1. How long have you worked here?

The CNA's answer to this question provides another statistic to contribute to the rate of staff turn-over in this nursing home.

The specific answer of the CNA is important also. It indicates the daily working conditions and the conditions under which care is provided to the residents. As a general rule, turn-over among the CNA is higher than that of the rest of the staff. There are many reasons why a CNA, in particular, leaves the employment of a nursing home. The first is a heavy caseload. Ideally, a CNA should be assigned approximately 7 residents. However, in many nursing homes that assignment escalates as high as 15 depending on how short staffed the nursing home is on that particular day. For example, Today the weather is warm and sunny for the first time in two weeks which corresponds with several CNAs calling in sick. No attempt is made to call in substitute CNAs to cover this shortage so the CNAs who do show up for work are assigned a heavier caseload than usual, resulting in frustrated employees and poor care for the residents.

A CNA may leave the employment of a nursing home due lack of action from the charge nurse when they are notified of a problem with a resident. For example, the CNA noticed a bed sore on Mr. Emery's foot when she got him out of bed this morning. She immediately informed the charge nurse who informs her that she will examine the wound in a few minutes and to continue dressing him. Feeling confident in her handling of the situation, the CNA follows these directions. The next morning the same CNA notices the same bed sore on Mr. Emery's foot only today it is twice the size and depth that it had been yesterday. Again, she informs the same charge nurse and receives the same directions which she follows. The third morning the she notices that today the sore on Mr. Emery's foot is down to the bone. She immediately informs the charge nurse on duty. This charge nurse is substituting for the regular charge nurse who is off today. The new charge nurse stops what she is doing and examines the wound. She contacts the physician for medication and treatment instructions and contacts the family to inform them of the wound. Finally, Mr. Emery will receive the kind of attention he needs.

2. What formal training qualifies you for this kind of work?

This answer highlights her medical training. As mentioned earlier, most nurses' aides have high school diplomas or the equivalent and have attended a seven week course in nurses' aide training, followed by a written certification exam. With this certification, she acquires the title of Certified Nurses' Aide and is qualified to work in a nursing home, providing general care to the residents. No continuing education training is required.

3. How many residents are in your care today?

The answer to this question directly reflects the amount of time given to each of those residents. Obviously, this answer should be a low number, so the CNA can take better care of all of the residents for whom they are responsible. Ideally, this number should be seven or less and should depend primarily upon the level of independence of each of those residents in providing their own care. For example, a CNA named Martha has been assigned 6 residents all of whom are able to dress themselves if their clothes are laid out on their beds. A CNA named Sandy on the other hand has been assigned 6 residents all of whom require Sandy to dress them completely. Sandy's residents require more of her time and assistance while Martha stands idle waiting for her residents to finish dressing. These residents should be assigned more equally between Martha and Sandy to ensure that all of the residents receive the care they need without overworking the CNAs.

While the abilities of the residents is a factor in their care, as demonstrated in the above example, the number of residents assigned to each CNA is also a factor. In many nursing homes each aide is responsible for providing care for as many as 15 residents simultaneously. In this situation, no resident is given the care they need, since it is impossible for one aide to keep up with the needs of so many residents. This unmanageable caseload results in an overworked, frustrated aide and the further decline in the quality of care for the residents. A high rate of staff turnover can be expected in of nursing home with this management practice.

Social Service Director
This individual is given a variety of titles in the nursing home industry. In some nursing homes, they are

referred to as the social service director, admissions coordinator, admissions director, and a variety of other titles. A nursing home which bestows on this person the title of admissions coordinator or admissions director is suspect for failure to discharge their residents back home. It would appear that these nursing homes emphasize admissions without pursuing discharge as a goal for their qualified residents.

Education
This person should have at least a four year college degree and experience working in the nursing home industry. They should be licensed by the state in which they practice but not all states issue these licenses. Therefore, this individual social worker may or may not have a state license.

Responsibilities
Regardless of their title, this individual is essentially a Social Worker. It is their responsibility to arrange for the admission and discharge of residents and to function as an advocate for the residents' rights. They may also provide mental health services depending upon their area of expertise and the needs of the residents.

During the admissions process, s/he should assist the resident and family to make any necessary arrangements with the hospital for this transfer and assist with any paperwork which might be required. S/he is responsible for educating the family regarding the application process and guidelines for Medicaid and other financial assistance programs.

The psychological and emotional well-being of the residents and their families is an ongoing concern for the social worker which begins during the admissions process with their adjustment to a new living situation and continues through the entirety of their stay. Safeguarding the residents basic human rights come under the auspice of the social worker as well, so each resident can enjoy the same rights and privileges inside the nursing home as they enjoyed in their own home. This is a lofty ideal which rarely comes to fruition even for a brief time.

Since nursing home residents usually stay there until their death, the only discharge duties required of the social worker is paperwork. If a nursing home is well-operated and oriented toward the welfare of their residents, there will be an active discharge process in place. In this rare situation, the social worker interacts frequently with the rehab staff in arranging for the successful discharge of those qualified residents. This will include housing, adaptive equipment, meals on wheels, housekeeping assistance, and visiting nurses.

Scams

Federal and state regulations require each nursing home to provide social services to their residents. However, this regulation is so vague that the administrator satisfies it by hiring one social worker to serve the entire building regardless of its size. Since most nursing facilities have over 100 residents, it is quite common to find one social worker serving all of them. Obviously, this is impossible for one individual so the residents are neglected due to understaffing.

This excessive work and understaffing has many other repercussions both to the residents and their families. There is no time for the social worker to assist the family with the admissions paperwork so s/he provides a packet of forms with no instructions or assistance leaving the family to muddle through on their own. There is no time to educate the family on Medicaid guidelines or assist with the application process so s/he advises them to call the state welfare office for assistance. There is no time for discharge planning of qualified residents to everyone stays for the remainder of their lives regardless of their abilities or their potential to live independently at home.

Interview Questions

Since the social worker is charged with the responsibility of assisting the residents and their families, s/he should be asked the following questions:

1. Will you assist with the admissions process?
2. Will you assist with Medicaid applications?
3. Are there established visiting hours?
4. Can the residents decorate their own room with personal belongings?
5. Does this nursing home have a residents' council?
6. Does the residents' council influence decisions concerning resident life?
7. Does the nursing home have a family council?
8. Does the family council influence decisions concerning resident life?
9. Are there private areas for residents to meet with their visitors or physician?

The answers to these questions will reveal the quality of care and assistance received by the resident and their family from the social worker.

1. Will you assist with the admissions process?

Assisting family members with the admissions process and the necessary paperwork is a primary duty, but as the only social worker in the building, s/he does not have time for this tutorial. Therefore, the family or legal representative is handed a stack of forms to complete on their own. This is the admissions packet. Among these forms you should find information concerning Advance Directives, Limited **Power of Attorney**, Wills, and the Admissions Contract. These are serious legal issues which should be discussed at length with your attorney before signing anything.

Advance Directives are instructions for the physician and family members regarding medical and life-sustaining measures which the resident wishes to be taken, in the event of life-threatening illness or accident.

Limited Power of Attorney is the assignment of authority to a family member or friend to act on the behalf of the resident in the event that the resident is unable to act or make decisions on his own behalf.

A Will is a legal document consisting of instructions regarding the financial or material assets of the resident in the event of their death.

The Admission's Contract is a legally binding document between the nursing home and the resident or their legal representative. It specifies the conditions under which the resident will live in this building. The Admission's Contract should include all of the following items:

- The resident's rights and obligations while living at this nursing home.
- Safeguards for those rights.
- Grievance procedure.
- The daily or monthly charge to live in the nursing home.

- Itemized price list of supplies and services not included in the basic charge.
- The nursing home's policy for holding a bed if you leave the nursing home temporarily for hospitalization or vacation.
- Certifications for Medicare and Medicaid programs.

    NOTE: If this nursing home is Medicare or Medicaid certified, it must accept Medicaid payments when a resident's personal funds run out, or accept Medicare payments if the resident qualifies. Discrimination against Medicaid recipients is illegal.

Before signing the admissions contract, make certain that it is complete with no blank spaces. If you disagree with any of the terms of the contract, you have the right to change them. However, if you make changes, each of them must be initialed by you and the nursing home representative. Due to complexities involved in the admissions process of some nursing homes and the lack of assistance from the social worker, it is best to consult your attorney. As always, request a copy of the entire admissions packet for future reference.

2. Will you assist with Medicaid applications?

Medicaid applications should be included in the admissions packet. However, if they are missing, ask the social worker for them. These forms should be readily available, and should be completed without delay if you anticipate that your loved one will require financial assistance. There may be a delay of several weeks or even months before receiving notification of your loved one's status for the Medicaid program, however if accepted the financial coverage will be effective on the date the application was submitted.

3. Are there established visiting hours?

Many nursing homes do not have established visiting hours. Visitors are welcome at any time in an effort to encourage frequent visits from family and friends. If this nursing home posts established visiting hours, request special arrangements to accommodate visitors at other times.

4. Can the residents decorate their own rooms with personal belongings?

As their home, each resident should be allowed to decorate their own room as they choose. This is one of their basic rights which they had when living outside a nursing home and which they retain when living inside a nursing home.

5. Does this nursing home have a residents' council?
6. Does the residents' council influence decisions concerning resident life?

A residents' council is a group of the residents chosen by the entire resident population to discuss concerns and issues pertinent to daily life within the nursing home. The chosen members are able to think clearly and communicate the needs and desires of the residents to the administration. As such, their opinions must be considered in those decisions which will ultimately affect their lives.

In reality, the recommendations of the residents' council are largely ignored by the administrator. The council exists because federal and state regulations mandate its existence but it is not taken seriously by the administration.

7. Does this nursing home have a family council?
8. Does the family council influence decisions concerning resident life?

The family council is a group of family members chosen from the families of all of the residents. Its function is to discuss issues and concerns regarding the lives of their loved ones in the nursing home and their decisions should influence daily life within the nursing home. This council is another mandate of federal and state regulations and exists as a result of this requirement.

As with the resident council, the family council and its decisions are largely ignored by the administration. At best, the concerns of the family council may be brought to the attention of the administrator but these concerns have no real impact upon the operations of the building or the daily living conditions of the residents.

Regardless of the futility of the resident and family councils, these entities are a requirement of state and federal regulations. As such if there is no resident or family councils, mark this nursing home off your list because they are in violation of state and federal regulations.

9. Are there private areas for residents to meet with their visitors or physician?

Since most nursing homes have two or three residents per room, the privacy and modesty of the residents must be safeguarded. For this reason, nursing homes must provide private areas for their residents to entertain visitors or to be examined by their physician. This right to privacy falls under the Basic Human Rights to which each resident is entitled by state and federal law.

The nursing home fails to provide private meeting areas and examination areas, the administration will advocate the use of the residents sleeping area with the curtain drawn, to serve this purpose. However, a curtain hardly satisfies the criteria for privacy.

Administrator

The administrator is business-oriented whose primary concern is the financial bottom line of the nursing home on any particular day. S/he is not interested in investing money in the improvement of the building to reap greater financial gains at a later date, since that requires spending money today. Improvements to the building and staff are completed only when forced by the federal and state investigators at the risk of closure.

Education

This individual is required to have a 4 year college degree but this degree could be in nursing, psychology, business, etc. The laws of most states do not specify a major field of education and no health care experience is required. S/he is required to obtain a state administrators license by passing a licensure examination in their state of employment. This license must be displayed in a prominent location at his place of employment so look for it.

Responsibilities

The nursing home administrator has many responsibilities to many different groups of people. S/he is responsible to the residents to provide good care from properly trained staff members; To the state surveyors for the compliance with all of the OBRA and state regulations; To the corporate owners to operate the nursing home in a cost-effective manner; and To the staff to provide safe working conditions and to support continuing education. In short, the administrator is a business man who must operate the nursing home in such a way as to comply with the regulations and provide a high quality of care for the residents while maintaining an acceptable bottom line.

Scams

As with any business, balancing quality and cost is not an easy task. The administrator who accomplishes this is somewhat of an unsung hero since failure results in poor care for the residents. Problems arise when the administrator and corporate owners allow money to completely rule their decisions.

There are many methods used by the corporate owners and the administrator to cut costs with no regard for the care of their residents. It is important to familiarize yourself with these methods so you will be able to identify them during your tour.

The first method can be easily detected upon entering the building. Federal and state law requires the administrator's license to be displayed in a prominent location for public view. However, it is common to display the license of regional director of the corporation while a student runs the building. This is acceptable if the student is adequately supervised by their regional administrator but in most cases they are not. This student is commonly referred to as an **AIT** or **Administrator In Training** and is not licensed or qualified to run a nursing home.

Health care equipment is frequently targeted for cost cutting measures and is most common in the rehab departments. An example of this was mentioned earlier in this text and involved the recycling of lead pipe. In this nursing home, lead pipe was removed from the plumbing system due to the risk of lead poisoning. However, this same pipe was later used to construct a crude set of parallel bars for the physical therapy department. The risk of lead poisoning through the tap water was replaced by the risk of lead poisoning through touch for those residents receiving physical therapy. These parallel bars were also too narrow for a wheelchair to fit between them so the resident was at risk for a fall with each use. Safe properly constructed parallel bars are adjustable both in height and width.

The most serious example of unsafe equipment and one which is commonly overlooked, involves the wheelchairs in which the residents sit every day. The nursing home is required to supply a wheelchair to those residents who need one but those chairs are damaged and unsafe. The vinyl seats and backs are cracked and torn resulting in scratches and cuts on the residents' fragile skin. The brakes of these wheelchairs no longer lock the wheels, so the chair rolls away as they try to stand up or sit down. The resident falls to the floor bring with them anyone who was trying to lend assistance.

Continuing education of the staff in a more subtle method of cutting costs. With the continuous breakthroughs in medical research, it is vital to the health of our senior citizens that all staff members responsible for their care update their training periodically. However, these courses cost money and administrators do not like to spend money. If an LPN requests time off to attend a continuing education course, that request will be denied since continuing education is not a universal requirement for LPN annual license renewal. The only instance in which her request will be granted is if she is employed in one of the few states which require LPNs to attend these courses to renew their license.

The LPN is not alone in this education dilemma. The RNA is also a target. As mentioned previously, the RNA is assigned to perform maintenance exercises with the residents rather than providing general care like the CNAs. Ideally, the RNAs should attend an eight week training course in Restorative Nursing Techniques, however usually refuses this request for education. Due to the cost and length of this course, the individual RNA is unable to pay the registration fee or take time off work to attend. Therefore, the RNA remains untrained for the duties assigned to her.

The most common victim of this education dilemma is the PT. She must renew her license annually and one of the requirements is continuing education. For this reason, the request of the PT for time off to attend the required courses is not refused outright, like the requests of the LPN and RNA.

As mentioned previously, the administrator to makes it very difficult for the PT to attend these courses by insisting on the following conditions:

1. Time off will not be paid.
2. No assistance with registration fees.
3. You must arrange for a replacement PT for your time away.

The first two conditions pose an obvious financial burden on the therapist but the last is frequently impossible especially for those therapists working in rural areas. If a replacement is located, this therapist must be approved by the administrator and arrangements made for their temporary employment. By the time all of these conditions are met, the deadline for registration for the course has passed. As a result, most physical therapists schedule courses for weekends or vacation time and pay the registration fee themselves.

Staff down-sizing is a cost-cutting method which has repercussions for the residents and the remaining staff since the number of residents requiring care stays the same. When the number of CNAs is cut, each CNA is assigned more residents. The workload of the CNA goes up and the quality of care for the residents goes down.

In times of low census, the PT will be contracted out to another nursing home part-time. This may work when both nursing homes have low census and few residents for the PT to treat, but when the census of either building goes back up, there are too many residents for one therapist to treat. In addition, the residents are divided between different locations, requiring travel time.

Some ruthless administrators have camouflaged this problem by directing the RNAs to perform the evaluations and treatments using the PT to supervise their work. This includes evaluations of resident wheelchairs, walking abilities, and equipment needs such as walkers and canes. These duties are far beyond the skills of the

RNA and it is illegal for anyone but a licensed therapist to perform them. It also poses a risk for injury and death for the resident. These safety issues should outweigh the cost but to many administrators cost is paramount, safety is neglected.

In the interest of boosting his bottom line, an administrator will utilize whatever means available with insurance fraud being the most common. One method is to bill the maintenance exercises performed by the RNA as if they were skilled physical therapy treatments performed by the PT. Unlike skilled physical therapy, these maintenance exercises are not covered by Medicare or other private insurance since they do not meet the requirements. However, the administrator can easily include the RNA programs with the billing information of the PT treatments and send all of it to Medicare for reimbursement. Unless the Medicare reviewer scrutinized these claims closely, it will not be detected. In addition, the Medicare reviewers are frequently overworked themselves, so few claims are scrutinized and the administrator is not likely to be caught.

The following example is an example of treating a patient based on her ability to pay. Mrs. Cromwell is a nursing home resident whose total care is currently being covered by Medicare Part A. Her condition is complex but she continues to improve everyday. In a staff meeting this morning, the administrator informs the staff that Mrs. Cromwell will exhaust her 100 days of Medicare benefits tomorrow. Since her secondary insurance does not pay as well, she will be discharged from the Medicare section and all therapies will stop. Upon hearing this the charge nurse protests that Mrs. Cromwell is doing extremely well and is expected to go back home within the next two weeks. The PT protests that without continued therapy Mrs. Cromwell will get worse and will have to remain in the nursing home. Unmindful of this information, the administrator replies that the decision is made and Mrs. Cromwell will be discharged from all Medicare services tomorrow. Although this is a blatant disregard for the resident and for the professional recommendations of the medical staff, the administrator has the final decision.

The most abhorrent example of cost cutting stems from the administrators own inadequacies when negotiating with the Medicare intermediary for a reimbursement rate which will cover all of the services required by the resident. If the administrator fails in this endeavor, the intermediary will pay only the contracted rate and the nursing home loses the rest. The following example will illustrate the consequences of these kinds of situations.

Mr. Andrews was in the hospital covered by Medicare Part A and needed nursing home placement. He was recovering from a massive stroke and required extensive services from the nursing and therapy departments. The skills of the nursing home staff was such that they were able to provide for all of the needs of this patient, however the administrator was concerned about his bottom line. The estimated cost to care for Mr. Andrews was $200 per day, but the maximum re-imbursement rate negotiated with the intermediary was $100 per day so the nursing home would lose $100 for each day Mr. Andrews was on Medicare Part A in this nursing home. As a result the administrator to refused to admit Mr. Andrews. Although Mr. Andrews needed complex care which this nursing home could provide, the administrator has the final decision.

Interview Questions

Below you will find a list of questions to ask the administrator followed by a detailed discussion of each one. All of the information involved in the answers to these questions readily available to the administrator, located in his office or elsewhere in the building.

1. How long have you worked here?
2. How much does Medicare reimburse the facility per resident?
3. How long does Medicare coverage last?
4. What is the room rate?
5. What services and supplies does this rate cover?
6. How much does Medicaid reimburse the facility per resident?
7. What services and supplies does this rate cover?
8. How long does Medicaid coverage last?
9. How many falls occurred in this building last month?
10. How many medical doctors come to this nursing home?
11. What other health professionals come to this nursing home?
12. How much does each of these services cost?
13. What precautions does the nursing home take to ensure the health of the residents during extreme weather?
14. What emergency provisions are stored here, in the event of a power outage?
15. Is the nursing home air-conditioned?
16. Are the residents allowed to smoke? Where?
17. Do you provide transportation to and from doctor's appointments?

18. Do you provide special services, such as ventilators and feeding tubes?
19. What is your policy regarding the purchase of prescription medications from our own pharmacist?
20. If my loved ones require hospitalization, to which hospital will they be sent?
21. Will their bed be available upon their return?
22. Is there a charge to hold the bed?
23. How much advance notice do you provide regarding an increase in the nursing home charges?
24. Does this nursing home accept special needs residents, such as Alzheimer's, or Aids?
25. Is the staff trained to care for these special residents?
26. Ask for references.

These questions will reveal information pertaining to the financial operation of the building, the quality of professional services, emergency preparedness and specialized services. A qualified administrator will know the answers to each of these questions so if s/he refuses to share this information or attempts to mislead you with vague or false information, mark them off your list and move on.

1. How long have you worked here?

The relevance of this question is two-fold: as contributing data for the turnover rate; and as the administrator's employment history. Since the administrator is a nursing home employee, his answer to this question when combined with the answers from other interviewed staff, will indicate the rate of staff turn-over for this nursing home.

The administrator's answer to this question warrants particular scrutiny, since he is professionally responsible for every occurrence which takes place within the nursing home. If the nursing home had a problem of some kind or if a serious incident occurs, the administrator is held responsible by state officials. He could lose his job or his administrator's license.

This level of responsibility provides a unique opportunity for the corporate owners to use the administrator as their scapegoat. In the event of a serious incident, the corporation will blame the administrator and fire him, even if the incident was beyond his control. The corporation expects the administrator to control all aspects of the nursing home, including the staff, residents and events to prevent incidents which might be harmful to their reputation. The most harmful incident is one which attracts the attention of the media or government officials such as a resident wandering off the premises. When incidents of this caliber occur, the corporation views it as the failure of the administrator to properly control his nursing home and fires him.

A common example of this draws upon the state survey information discussed in a previous chapter. If a nursing home has too many level A violations during a state survey and is put in stop placement, the administrator is fired to pacify the state survey team.

This scapegoat strategy was used in 1991 when an incident of deliberate violation of a resident's Basic Human Rights was publicized. Mrs. Taylor suffered from confusion with mental delusions and developed the habit of taking things which did not belong to her. She wandered into staff offices and residents' rooms collecting items of interest to her. Obviously, this was upsetting for the residents and staff. In an attempt to change this behavior, the director of nurses and the **corporate nurse consultant** designed a behavior modification program. (A corporate nurse consultant is a nurse employed by the corporate owners to advise and assist the nursing staff.)

Their behavior modification program was similar to the time-out plan used with children. Under this program, the nursing home staff was instructed to take Mrs. Taylor to her room for five minutes whenever she acted out with this behavior. When Mrs. Taylor's family became aware of this, they were justifiably alarmed. They were outraged that the nursing home staff would treat their mother and grandmother like a child, rather than respect her as an adult. This behavior modification program was punitive in nature, violated this resident's rights, and could be considered abusive. In response to a complaint from Mrs. Taylor's family, the state survey team arrived to investigate this incident of resident abuse.

The corporate owners and the corporate nurse consultant denied all knowledge of the incident. All responsibility was placed squarely on the shoulders of the administrator and the director of nurses. The corporate owners fired that administrator and director of nurses and drafted a formal apology to the State governing body, Mrs. Taylor, and her family.

Although the corporate nurse consultant was involved in the design and implementation of this behavior modification program, the corporation's use of the administrator and director of nurses as scapegoats successfully avoided a probable lawsuit.

2. How much does Medicare reimburse the facility per resident?

The reimbursement plan for Medicare Part A is fundamentally different from the reimbursement plan for Medicare Part B. For patients covered by Medicare Part A, the nursing home is reimbursed at a single rate for all of the patient's care, including all rehabilitation services. For example, John Doe is transferred to a nursing home from a hospital after suffering from a fractured hip. The nursing home may be reimbursed by the intermediary at a rate of $100 a day. This $100 includes all aspects of his care, such as room and board, medications and bandages, physical therapy, occupational therapy, and the use of medical equipment such as a wheelchair or walker.

In addition, this rate of reimbursement was negotiated and a contract signed between the nursing home and the intermediary, so if the cost of Mr. Doe's care is $150 per day, the nursing home is only reimbursed at the contracted daily rate of $100. Since the contracted reimbursement rate insufficient to cover the actual cost of care, the nursing home loses $50 per day for each day Mr. Doe is on Medicare Part A.

Under Medicare Part B, rehabilitation services are ancillary, which means that the treatments are billed and reimbursed separately from the general care of the resident. The general care is reimbursed on a per-resident basis. Rehabilitation services, such as PT, OT and SLP are reimbursed for the units of time required to treat the resident and is calculated using the formula: One unit equals 15 minutes.

For instance, a PT spends 45 minutes treating a resident which is the equivalent of three units of time.

The nursing home's reimbursement rate is $20 per unit, so the nursing home is paid a total of $60 for the three units of time spent by the PT.

An administrator who is oriented toward rehabilitation knows his building's rate of reimbursement per unit. An administrator who is not oriented toward rehabilitation does not know the answer without looking it up or is unaware of the Medicare Part B ancillary reimbursement program.

3. How long does Medicare coverage last?

The answer to this question is very simple and every nursing home administrator should know this answer without having to research it. Individuals covered by Medicare Part A have 100 days of complete coverage, beginning from the date of their admission to the hospital. Medicare Part B has no time limit but allows full rehabilitation services so long as the resident shows progress in a reasonable and predictable fashion.

4. What is the room rate?

Your tour guide should volunteer this information but if they do not, the administrator is the individual to ask.

Many nursing homes operate on a basic per day room rate while other facilities especially those which are corporate-owned, have changed their rate structure. These nursing homes require the resident to "buy in" to the corporation at a one-time, extremely-high down payment. After this exorbitant initial fee, the resident receives the usual monthly bill for room and board. This similar to a home mortgage in that there is a large down payment followed by years of monthly payments.

However, in this arrangement the mortgage is never paid off. The resident continues to pay until they die without gaining possession of anything.

Corporations use this arrangement when they own a variety of nursing homes which admit residents requiring various amounts of care. Some of these buildings are classified as Skilled Nursing Facilities, commonly known as nursing homes which provide total care for their residents. Other buildings are classified as Assisted Living Facilities, designed for individuals requiring minimal assistance. Still other buildings are classified as Retirement Homes for those requiring no assistance at all.

On the surface, this sounds like an ideal situation since as your health improves or deteriorates, you can move from one type of home to another without leaving the corporation. The current trend is for corporate-owned buildings to have all of these different levels of care available in the same building or private community. It is a tempting offer to have your home secure and all of your needs provided for the rest of your life.

The security of this arrangement were factual, it would be very attractive but the reality is rather grim. An example of this is Seascape Retirement Community which has a **skilled nursing facility, assisted-living** and retirement apartments, all conveniently located within one large building. The residents who "buy in" to this building pay a one-time down payment in excess of $50,000. Most of these residents sell their own homes to pay this fee. Then they are billed a monthly room rate for the remainder of their lives. This arrangement puts the corporation in the position of life-time landlord and the resident as a captive tenant. If a resident has a bad experience in the building or wants to leave for other reasons, she is unable to move since she sold her home and invested the proceeds with her "landlord".

Another problem with this arrangement is that nursing homes go out of business everyday. If this corporate-owned building went out of business or was sold to another corporation, all of these residents stand a good chance of losing their entire investment and their homes. In reality, a lifetime "buy-in" arrangement is not secure at all. It is a lie perpetrated by ruthless business-men to victimize unsuspecting senior citizens and to relieve them of their lifesaving's.

5. What services and supplies does the room rate cover?

The quote you receive for the room rate does not cover all services and supplies required by the residents. The room rate typically covers general care by the CNA, assistance bathing and the use of a wheelchair. Services not covered include laundry, podiatry care, hearing exams, vision exams, dental care, hair cuts and hair styling. Supplies which are not provided include over-the-counter drugs, personal hygiene products, hearing aids, hearing aid batteries, glasses, and dentures.

Any one of these services or perhaps all of them will be necessary for the proper care of your loved one and they can be very expensive, so you need to know who pays for them. Get a list of all services and products which are included in the room rate and those which are not included. Also, question if the resident may leave the nursing home to receive these services. Your regular dentist or hair stylist may be less expensive than those contracted into the facility.

6. How much does Medicaid reimburse the facility per resident?

All nursing homes which participate in the Medicaid program have a fixed reimbursement rate per resident. For example, Pleasant Valley Nursing Home has a Medicaid reimbursement rate of $50 per resident. This $50 must cover the cost a residents total care for every resident covered by Medicaid. Since Medicaid is governed by individual states, this reimbursement plan will vary depending upon where you live. This rate typically includes room and board, nursing, rehabilitation, podiatry, dental and vision care. Adaptive equipment, such as a wheel chair, special eating utensils, walkers and canes are also included in this single rate. This single rate is meant to provide for all of the needs of the resident. Unfortunately, the amount of money which the nursing home is reimbursed is the same for all of the residents with no consideration for their varied functional abilities or their diverse needs.

Pleasant Valley Nursing Home provides a clear example of this variation in resident needs and abilities. Mr. Abbott and Mr. Zeller are covered by Medicaid. Pleasant Valley Nursing Home is reimbursed by Medicaid $50 for each of these two residents. Mr. Abbott walks independently and requires no assistance except with medications. However, Mr. Zeller suffers from numerous medical conditions requiring a vast number of medications administered by the nurse. He also requires a feeding tube, the assistance of two CNAs to get out of bed, and adaptive equipment from the physical therapist. While the daily reimbursement of fifty dollars may cover the cost of care for Mr. Abbott, the cost of caring for Mr. Zeller will obviously be more than that. Therefore,

Pleasant Valley Nursing Home's financial accounting for Mr. Zeller is in the red. If this happens too frequently, Pleasant Valley Nursing Home will be out of business. Since this $50 does not cover all of the services required by Mr. Zeller, the nursing home will bill his family for some of the services and supplies required for his care.

Since the nursing home is bound by state regulations to provide all necessary services and equipment with an insufficient reimbursement rate from Medicaid, it is not surprising that most nursing homes operate in or near the red. In addition, senior citizens are living longer and requiring more intensive care which eventually depletes even their lifesaving's making Medicaid the only option for the majority of them. This puts the nursing home in a serious financial dilemma. A nursing home is a business and like any business, they must operate in the black in order to keep their doors open. Therefore, this insufficient reimbursement provides financial incentive for the nursing home to avoid admitting patients with complex conditions, or to avoid providing the services and equipment which their patients need.

7. What services and supplies does this Medicaid rate cover?

State regulations require the nursing home to provide for all of the need of the resident for a single reimbursement rate. Their family should receive no bill for extra services since all services and equipment should be included in the per resident Medicaid rate. However, the nursing home administrator will prey upon the familys' naivete regarding these regulations and bill them for the services in a attempt to recover his losses. Therefore, request a list of all services which are included in the rate and a list of services which are not.

8. How long does this Medicaid coverage last?

Once your relatives qualify for Medicaid, they will receive benefits for the remainder of their lives, unless there are changes in their financial status while they are alive. A common example is if their savings account exceeds the financial maximum limit to qualify for Medicaid. Simply, there is too much money. Here, some of the money must be spent to continue to qualify for Medicaid coverage.

9. How many falls occurred in this nursing home last month?

This will reveal if this nursing home is a safe living environment. The term "falls" refers to the number of times anyone fell in this nursing home. If the answer is five, this could mean five residents each of whom fell one time or it could mean one resident who fell five times. A good rule of thumb here is one or two falls for every 100 residents. If the number of falls is higher than that, there is a problem. The staff of this nursing home is not taking proper care of their residents. It may be that there are not enough employees to supervise all of the residents who are at risk for falling. The facility may have enough workers but they are not adequately trained. Another possibility is that the workers are lazy and are not be doing their jobs. Regardless of the reason, the result is the same: This nursing home is not safe. Mark it off your list and move on.

If the administrator is unwilling to answer s/he will attempt to divert your attention by stating that he does not have this information. This is a lie. She must have these statistics readily available because each fall must be appropriately reported to the state. Therefore, under the Freedom of Information Act, this information is available to you.

10. How many medical doctors come to this nursing home?

In order to give an exact answer to this question, the administrator may need to do a small amount of research. However, if the administrator is actively involved in the operation of this nursing home, he will be able to give you an accurate estimate.

To ensure that your loved one receives the same quality of care inside the nursing home as they received while living outside the nursing home, ask their own physician if he will continue seeing them in the nursing home. If s/he refuses, you have no choice but to rely upon one of the physicians who attend to the residents here.

Get a list of the medical doctors who attend to residents in this nursing home and the number of residents which each physician visits. Although the administrator cannot divulge the names of those residents seen by each physician--that is confidential information--the number of patients seen by each physician can be shared. The physician with the highest number of residents is typically the **medical director** of the nursing home. Refer to chapter nine for the implications and ramifications of this arrangement.

11. What other health professionals come to this nursing home?

Other health professionals include a Speech-language Pathologist, an Occupational Therapist, a Podiatrist, a Dentist, a Dietitian, an Optometrist, and various Mental Health professionals. Ask for a list of these health professionals and a schedule of when each of them is expected to visit. A lengthy list would indicate that the needs of the residents are being met.

Specifically, the OT, like the PT, should visit five days per week. However, other professionals such as the optometrist and podiatrist will visit as seldom as once per month or less.

12. How much does each of these services cost?

Although each of the services mentioned above is necessary, they are seldom, if ever, free of charge. While these services should be included in the Medicaid rate, the ruthless administrator will prey upon the residents' families with a bill for these services.

This question addresses the financial concern of the cost of these services and whom is responsible for paying for them. If your loved one is currently covered by Medicare Part A, then all Physical, Occupational, and Speech-language therapy are covered as a part of their necessary rehabilitation services. However, the other services may or may not be covered by the private insurance which currently covers their medical needs. Ask the administrator for a fee schedule for these services. Expect him to know if any of these services are included in the room rate fee and if any of these services are covered by your relative's insurance company. In addition, the administrator should inform you as to who is responsible for paying for those necessary services which are not covered by insurance. You have the right and the financial need to know this information.

13. What precautions does the nursing home take to ensure the health of the residents during extreme weather?

Regardless of where you live, there is some extreme weather common to the area. Every facility must make preparations and have their procedures in place, in order to withstand these conditions. In addition, extreme weather is frequently accompanied by power outages so the nursing home must be prepared for this hardship as well.

14. In the event of a power outage, what emergency provisions are stored here?

This issue is not only regulated by state law, but is potentially life threatening. It is a critical question regardless of where you live, since power outages are not specific to any part of the country.

According to state laws, each nursing home is required at all times to have emergency supplies such as emergency lightening, a supply of drinking water, generator-powered electrical wall outlets for emergency equipment, and a battery powered radio with batteries. However, most nursing homes fail to store these critical items. The following scenario describes one such nursing home.

On the Presidential Inauguration Day of 1993, the Pacific Northwest was hit by the windstorm of the century. Several hours of 50 to 70 mile per hour winds resulted in widespread power outages throughout several counties. Unfortunately, Seascape Nursing Home had taken none of the precautions mandated by state law. The emergency lighting was only in the hallways. There was natural light coming in the windows of some of the residents' bedrooms, but since it was already late in the afternoon, that light was fading fast. There was no battery-powered radio to get emergency information or a weather forecast. There was no heat and no stored supply of drinking water.

This was a serious situation in January. It was fortunate for everyone that one staff member carried emergency supplies in her car. The administrator used her portable radio to listen for emergency and weather information and the nurses' aides took turns using her two flashlights to care for the residents. With these few emergency supplies, the situation was far from satisfactory, but without them it could have been disastrous.

One factor which compounded this situation occurred when the local police and fire departments stopped by to offer their assistance. In an effort to hide his lack of preparedness, the administrator refused their offers assuring them that this nursing home was quite prepared for this type of emergency. Therefore, the staff was left to provide the best care they could, in a poorly supplied nursing home, during a prolonged power outage, in January just to hide the incompetence of their administrator.

15. Is the building air conditioned?

This is critical if you live in an area which experiences severe heat for extended periods. Air conditioning can do much to safeguard the lives and health of the residents of many nursing homes across the country during the hot summer. For example, during the summer of 1995, in Chicago and the surrounding areas, over 300 people died from heat related conditions. Many of them were senior citizens.

16. Are the residents allowed to smoke? Where?

Many nursing homes are now considered smoke free with a ban on smoking inside the building. However, the residents retain the right to smoke even if it against their doctors advice. Most businesses solve this problem by allowing their employees to smoke outside on their lunch hour or during breaktime. However, these residents are physically unable to go outside without assistance. In this situation, a location must be designated for the residents who smoke. This area may be outside, but it must be easily accessible to wheelchairs and sheltered from the weather.

17. Do you provide transportation to and from doctor's appointments?

Nursing home administrators have negotiated contracts with certain doctors and other health care professionals to provide services to their residents. While the resident retains the right to see whatever service provider they choose, it is the desire of the nursing home administrator that their residents avail themselves of these services even if they are more expensive. To that end, the nursing home will not provide transportation to these other service providers but will make the necessary arrangements with an independent transportation service if the resident insists. The fee for this door to door transportation service ranges from nominal to exorbitant giving clear financial incentive for the resident to accept the services of one of the nursing home's contracted providers.

18. Do you provide special services, such as ventilators or feeding tubes?

These special services require a higher level of skill from those nurses assigned to care for these residents. These nurses must be appropriately trained in the techniques of operating this specialized equipment as well as caring of these seriously ill residents. The provision of these services also requires more licensed nurses to be on the premises during every shift than the standard regulations mandate.

19. What is your policy regarding my purchase of prescription medications from my own pharmacist?

Many nursing homes will not allow a family member to bring in medications of any kind. In addition, they will not allow the residents to keep any medication or vitamins in their own possession. This is a legitimate safety concern since it is common for a resident to wander into another resident's room and rummage through personal belongings in drawers and closets placing that resident at risk of ingesting medications by mistake. While the nursing home administration is responsible for enforcing safeguards against this invasion, it remains a frequent occurrence.

The financial incentive behind this policy of no personal medications is the contract which frequently exists between the nursing home and a local pharmacy to provide all medications used in the nursing home. Although over the counter medications can be obtained at the local grocery store for a fraction of the cost, the nursing home must purchase them from the pharmacy. This inflated cost is then billed to the resident or to Medicare/Medicaid.

20. If my loved one requires hospitalization, to which hospital will they be sent?

Nursing homes administrators have an unwritten agreement or even a formal contract with a specific hospital. The hospital agrees to discharge their elderly patients to this nursing home and the nursing home agrees to send their ill residents to that hospital. This arrangement ensures both the hospital and nursing home of a source for patient admissions. Neither the patient nor their family is consulted in this matter which smacks of a human rights violation.

21. Will their bed be available upon their return?
22. Is there a charge to hold the bed?

When your loved one goes to the hospital, the nursing home may or may not hold their bed in anticipation of their return. If the nursing home is full, they are less likely to hold the bed since it could be filled immediately with a new admission. However, if the nursing home has several vacancies, they are more likely to accommodate your need to hold the bed in order to ensure the admission. If the nursing home is willing to hold your loved one's bed during their absence, be prepared to pay a bed-hold fee. This is a daily fee which should be less that the standard room rate. If this nursing home charges a bed-hold fee, the specific fee schedule should be included in the admissions contract.

23.   How much advance notice do you provide regarding an increase in the charges?

Every nursing home should give advance written notice of any change in their charges. The time requirement should be specified in the admission contract. If you do not receive a written notice, insist to the administrator that the increased bill will be acknowledged as that written notice so you will begin paying the increased rate at the next billing period. This will ensure that the administrator does not make this mistake again.

24.   Does this nursing home accept special needs residents, such as Alzheimer's or Aids?

25.   Is the staff trained to care for these special residents?

These special residents require special services and a special environment. The staff, in direct contact with these patients, must be properly trained in their care and this training must be properly documented in their employee files. In addition, for Alzheimer's patients, the environment must be safe and secure, usually requiring a locked wing adapted especially for them. This enables them to wander freely about the secured area in complete safety.

26. Ask for references.

This request will surprise most administrators since they seldom receive such requests. However, he should be able to give you a list of family members of other residents who will attest to the quality of care provided in this nursing home. If he cannot give you such a list, mark them off your list of candidate nursing homes and move on.

Director of Nurses

This person is responsible for the medical care of all of the residents in this nursing home but s/he has no direct contact with them. She provides no care to the residents and serves no purpose other than a managerial figurehead for the nursing department.

Although the laws of most states mandate that the Director of Nurses must be at least a Registered Nurse(RN), these credentials designate two, three, or four years of training depending upon the regulations of the particular state in which the nursing home is located. In a few of the better nursing homes, the Director of Nurses has a Bachelor of Science Degree in Nursing (BSN) which is a four year college degree. Unfortunately, since the minimum legal requirement of most states is an RN which commands a much lower salary, the ruthless administrator will hire a two year RN for the position of Director of Nurses instead of a more qualified BSN.

Survey Report

If no observation or interview on your tour has eliminated this facility from your list, then it is time to review their last survey report. All State survey reports are a matter of public record and the nursing home is required by law to keep a copy of their most recent survey report readily available for public review, so do not be dissuaded from this task.

This document will illuminate areas in which the nursing home has failed to provide adequate care to the residents, and identify recurring problems which the nursing home has failed to address. Moreover, it will provide information regarding violations from the previous survey which remain uncorrected.

Size

Your review of this document actually begins before you open it. The rule of thumb for all survey reports is: the thicker the document, the worse the survey. This is true because the greater the number and seriousness of the violations found by the survey team, the more text the team was required to write.

Indicators

At the beginning of the report are several pages containing the signatures of the administrator and corporate owners. Following these pages is a summary listing the number of level A and level B violations. Each of these regulations is identified by an indicator which in some states is called an **F-tag** and should be carefully reviewed. If you consider any of these violations to be potentially life threatening, mark this candidate off your list and move on.

Upon opening this portion of the report, it may be necessary to turn it lengthwise (landscape view). The surveyors and reviewers of some states of some states prefer this presentation over the standard portrait view as found with most documents and books. Regardless of the presentation, along the left margin you will find the indicator or tag numbers. The state of Washington for example numbers their F-tags using the form of F000 so the F-tags for Specialized Rehabilitative Services are F356, F357, and F358. Each of the tag numbers from the list of violations is discussed in the narrative portion of the report. These Washington "F tags" should be very similar to the system used by other states since the survey process of each state must comply with federal mandates.

Common Violations

The most common violations refer to nutrition and meal preparation. One nursing home received a citation for having the temperature of the refrigerators set at 44 degrees. This temperature was too warm, resulting in spoilage and food poisoning among the residents. Another common violation involving meals occurs when a resident is given the incorrect type of food. For example, Mr. Brown was a 76 year old gentleman who propelled himself around in a wheelchair without the aid of the staff. He had difficulty chewing and swallowing solid food but he was able to feed himself. One afternoon he was served a peanut butter and jelly sandwich as an afternoon snack. He took his sandwich over to his usual place by a corner window to eat it. Approximately fifteen minutes later, the nurse approached him to give him his afternoon medications. He didn't respond when she called his name and as she turned his chair around he slumped over the armrest, his face a bluish-gray. With the assistance of several other staff members, she was able to resuscitate him but he suffered extensive mental damage. Clearly, this was negligence and malpractice. Mr. Brown was given the wrong type of food, choked and died. There is no way of knowing exactly how long he was without oxygen but one thing is clear. He suffered brain damage through the negligence of the nursing home staff.

A high profile violation commonly reported in the media refers to residents who are unable to feed themselves being left unattended with a tray of food. When the CNA returns for the tray, she documents that the resident did not eat and takes the tray away. Although the negligence of this situation is clear, the resident is unable to report it.

Other common violations include giving a resident the wrong medication or neglecting to give the medications at all. For example, Nurse Baxter threw pills in the garbage instead of giving them to the appropriate resident. When she was caught, she was fired and lost her nurse's license.

Nurse Baxter's violation was intentional but the majority of medication errors are not. They are the result of carelessness and occur on a daily basis. It is not uncommon for a nurse to give the wrong medication seven to ten percent of the time. This dangerous situation necessitates that the resident's family become aware of the medications prescribed by the physician and which medications are actually given to their loved one.

The most appalling violation involves proper hygiene. The majority of nursing home residents are not provided with the proper bedding or turned in bed to prevent bedsores. They are left to lie in the same position all day on soiled sheets and in their own waste!

All of these instances of negligence and malpractice are finally getting the public attention they deserve. Nursing home conditions are a common topic for media attention and public outrage. More and more of these cases are being tried in court every year and there seems to be a growing empathy for our elderly. This is evident in the large verdicts being awarded by juries across the country.

Plan of Correction

After reviewing the listed violations, it is equally important to review the nursing home's **plan of correction**. This is the facility's response to the violations and their plan to correct them. These steps must be specific and understandable. The vague statement that a particular staff member will solve this problem is not sufficient. For example, at Merry Acres Nursing Home, the plan of correction for the violations read as follows: The PT will address the issue of residents being positioned poorly in bed; The dietitian will address the issue of meals which are prepared hot being served to the residents cold.

These staff members are considered **allied health professionals**. This term means that their services are available in addition to the standard doctors and nurses. This designation also places them outside of the jurisdiction of the State survey team. By turning the responsibility of the violations over to these allied health professionals, Merry Acres Nursing Home found a loophole in the state survey system and used it to avoid correcting the violations. That loophole is that by passing these violations off to allied health professionals, the state survey team was unable to re-survey to verify that these violations were corrected. In this way, Merry Acres avoided probable fines which would result from these uncorrected violations.

The nursing home's legal council can also be used to avoid correcting survey violations. In this maneuver, the nursing home administration charges their attorney with the task of writing a letter of rebuttal to the state survey department, refuting the listed violations. When faced with the threat of litigation, whether real, implied or imagined, the State will choose not to respond. Therefore, the letter of rebuttal takes the place of a plan of correction and the violations remain unaddressed and uncorrected. For example, Pleasant Hills Nursing Home received a citation for tying residents to their wheelchairs without the necessary consultations of medical staff and family, a clear violation of residents' rights. The administrator presented the nursing home's attorney with the task of rebutting this violation. A letter of rebuttal was drafted to the Department of Health refuting that at the last survey, Pleasant Hills Nursing Home was charged with the task of making the nursing home safe for all residents and chose restraints as a method to accomplish this. This letter which ended with the threat of litigation, was sent to the Department of Health with a copy in the survey report. When faced with this threat of litigation, the Department of Health responded by ignoring the situation. A plan of correction was not written, the abuse of restraints was not corrected and Pleasant Hills Nursing Home was not re-surveyed for corrections. In short, the Department of Health was scared off by the attorney.

Unscheduled Visit

If this facility withstands your scrutiny of all of the information you have acquired, they are a candidate for your unscheduled visit. This visit should be a day or two after your scheduled tour. Instead of calling ahead for an appointment, show up at the building unannounced. You need to see the daily operation of the building, not a special performance choreographed just for you. This visit should be early morning or late afternoon in order to overlap with a mealtime. For example, your tour of

Oak Ridge Nursing Home was completed yesterday. From the information acquired, you determined that this candidate may be your grandmother's future home. Breakfast is served from 8:00 to 9:30 each morning so you decided to visit the facility tomorrow morning at that time for an unscheduled tour.

The purpose of this brief tour is to view the facility in its daily routine. Is there any difference in the basic operation of the building today, compared to your last visit? If the answer is "no", then you are probably viewing the actual operation of nursing home. In this case, you can be confident that the information you accumulated on your scheduled tour is reliable. If there is a difference in the nursing home's routine today, then on your last visit you were shown a choreographed performance instead of seeing the actual operation of the nursing home. All of the information you collected on your scheduled tour is unreliable. Mark this candidate nursing home off your list, and move on.

Chapter Summary

Upon entering the building verify that the facility's license to operate and the administrator's professional license is displayed in a prominent location. This is required by state law. Furthermore, verify the individual acting as the building's administrator is the same person identified on the license.

Your scheduled tour will be conducted by the administrator, director of nurses, or a member of the marketing department. Regardless of the identity of this individual the goal of the tour guide is to emphasize the positive features of the facility while obscuring the negative. The tour guide is a salesperson trying to sell you, the customer, the services of their facility. Expect to tour high profile areas such as the nurses' station, dining room, physical therapy department, and a resident's room in the Medicare wing. Expect to be steered away from the Medicaid section which receives little staff attention and resources. Pertinent questions for the tour guide are listed and discussed in detail giving special attention to vague and misleading responses using factual examples to further illustrate vital information.

The physical therapist is a rehabilitation professional whose goal is to improve the strength and mobility of the resident. S/he has at least a four year Bachelor of Science degree in Physical Therapy and maintains her annual licensure through continuing education. S/he is responsible for administering Medicare A and B physical therapy benefits to all residents who qualify and educating the nursing home staff and families to improve resident care. Verify that the PT's professional license is conspicuously displayed; that this license is current and is issued for the state in which the nursing home is located.

Occasionally, a nursing home will hire a physical therapist whose only interest is collecting a paycheck without fulfilling their responsibilities or who succumbs to the administrator's coercion to discharge residents before they are functionally ready.

Physical Therapy Assistants are not licensed in every state and have no consistent regulations governing their practice. As a result of inadequate regulations, PTAs provide whatever services they choose without proper training and with no fear of repercussion. As with the PT, verify that the PTA's license is conspicuously displayed; that this license is current and is issued for the state in which the nursing home is located.

A list of pertinent interview questions for the physical therapist is followed by a detailed discussion of each. Vague and misleading responses are explained giving particular attention to violations in federal and state laws and insurance regulations. Factual examples are used to further illustrate issues of special import.

The RNA should be a certified as a nurse's aid, have attended an eight week course in restorative nursing techniques, and received on-the-job training from the PT, OT, and SLP. However, since there are no government or insurance regulations controlling this individual, there is no minimum education requirement and they provide whatever services the administrator directs them to provide regardless of their lack of training. The RNA is a frequently used pawn in the administrators game to improve his financial bottom line by whatever means necessary. However, due to insufficient training, the RNA is completely unaware of this.

Four questions directed toward the RNA are listed and explained in detail. Misleading and appropriate responses are discussed giving special attention to compliance with government regulations. Actual events are exemplified to clearly illustrate vital points.

The charge nurse is responsible for the medical care of all residents in her section and for supervising all care-giving staff caring for those residents. By law, the charge nurse must be an RN or LPN but these credentials are not consistently regulated from one state to the next. There is no consistent nationwide guarantee of minimum skill level among these nurses. Additionally, continuing education requirements vary from state to state, so there is no guarantee that the skills of this nurse are current.

The charge nurse must perform a thorough examination on any resident suffering a change in condition or functional status and consult with the physician, all appropriate allied health professionals, and the resident's family. These actions must be completely documented in the medical chart but the charge nurse rarely fulfills these obligations, especially near the end of her shift.

Methods employed by the charge nurse to avoid her responsibilities were described in detail using factual examples for clear illustration. Pertinent questions for the charge nurse are listed and discussed in detail with particular attention given to misleading language and responses.

The nurses' aide provides direct care to the residents in all of their activities such as dressing, grooming and personal hygiene. State and federal regulations require that nursing home nurses' aide be certified through the completion of a seven week training course culminating in an examination. This basic training should be enhanced by on-the-job training from the rehab staff and frequently updated through continuing education. Each CNA working in the general nursing home population should be assigned seven residents but they typically are assigned twice that number, resulting in neglect.

A short list of questions is included and discussed in detail to reveal information regarding the training and workload of the CNA.

The social service director is a social worker who is responsible for arranging for the admission of new residents, advocating for the resident's rights during their stay and arranging for their discharge when appropriate. This individual should have at least a four college degree with ongoing continuing education as well as experience in the nursing home industry and a license to practice within the state in which the nursing home is located. Excessive caseload and understaffing result in frequent neglect of responsibilities to the residents and their families. Questions aimed at revealing the quality of care and assistance received from the social worker are listed and discussed in detail. Particular attention is given to the admissions' packet and its contents.

The administrator is a business person whose primary concern is the building's financial bottom-line. S/he must have a four year college degree but the field of study is not specified so s/he could be a nurse, accountant, etc. The administrator operating the building must be licensed in the state in which the nursing home is located and displayed in a prominent location. The administrator is responsible for providing well trained staff to care for the residents, keeping the building in good repair, and operating the business in a cost effective manner without sacrificing quality care. Difficulties arise when the administrator concerns himself solely with the cost of running the business. Specific attention is afforded the cost-cutting scams most frequently utilized by these ruthless individuals. The purpose of administrator's interview questions is to reveal information regarding the operation of the building, quality of care of the residents, appropriate staffing and training of those staff members, in addition to emergency preparedness. Each of these questions is discussed in detail with factual examples to further illustrate the pertinent issues. Before ending this interview with the administrator, you want to ask for a list of references.

The director of nurses is responsible for the medical care of every resident in the nursing home but s/he has no direct contact with them and merely serves a figurehead leaving resident care issues to the charge nurses.

State law requires this individual to be an RN but this is a meaningless credential since the minimum requirement is only two years of training.

After the staff interviews, there is one task remaining before leaving the building: A review of the last survey report. This document illuminates areas in which the nursing home has failed to provide adequate care to the residents. The thicker the survey report, the worse the survey. All F-tag violations should be thoroughly reviewed. Common violations involve nutrition, food preparation, resident neglect and medication errors.

The plan of correction is also a target for review. This is the nursing home's plan to correct the violations identified by the survey team and prevent them from reoccurring. Particular attention is given to scams and loopholes used by to circumvent this survey process with factual examples for illustration.

The unscheduled visit should follow the tour by a few days and should be unannounced. The goal is to view the standard daily operation of the facility to test the validity of your previous observations.

Chapter 7
Marketing Strategies

I n this chapter you will learn the four basic advertising ploys used by nursing homes to market their services to emphasize their attributes while masking their problems.

You will also learn how a small portion of the regulations is take out of context and used to "sell" their services to the public and further the owners financial gains. Particular attention is given to false advertising.

Transitional Care Facility

Some nursing homes market themselves as **Transitional Care Facilities**. Their advertisements state that they have physical therapy, occupational therapy, and speech therapy, five or seven days per week; that they have skilled nursing by an RN or BSN available 24 hours per day, seven days per week. They even promote a secure Alzheimer's unit, and Hospice services. The key to this marketing strategy is promoting that the average length of stay for their residents is twenty days or less. This is intentionally designed to imply that anyone admitted to their facility recovers at this miraculous rate.

The advertised length of stay of 20 days or less is true but the advertisement does not state the location to which these residents are discharged. In addition you, as the consumer, are not told that Medicare Part A insurance coverage pays 100% of the bill for a patient's care for days 1 through 20. For days 21 through 100, Medicare Part A insurance coverage pays only 80% of the bill, so there is financial incentive to discharge every resident within the first 20 days. Unfortunately, the majority of residents do not fully recover in that short period of time and are discharged to another nursing home on day 21.

Another financial incentive which exists under this transitional care policy regards residents with severe conditions, such as a stroke. Someone who suffered a severe stroke will frequently be in the hospital for most of those first 20 days. Since there are very few days left for which Medicare will pay 100% of the bill, the transitional care facility refuses to admit them. Money is the determining factor in their admission procedures of whom is admitted and how long they can stay. If there is money readily available, the resident is admitted and they can stay until the money runs out.

Geriatric Rehabilitation Facility

Some nursing homes are advertised as **Geriatric Rehabilitation Facilities**. This type of building will house a sizable wing of rooms designated for Medicare Part A patients with rehabilitation potential. These are referred to as Medicare Certified Beds. It will also be home to a therapy department of adequate size and with all the appropriate equipment and supplies for physical, occupational, and speech therapy programs.

Appropriate equipment for a geriatric physical therapy program should consist of: a raised mat table which is padded; adjustable parallel bars; an overhead pulley system; a standing table; simulated staircase; simulated street curb; and cuff weights. Appropriate supplies include: straight-leg walkers, wheeled walkers, straight canes, canes with four points, and transfer belts. The physical therapy staff should consist of at least one full-time PT, a full-time PTA and two physical therapy aids.

The occupational therapy program should have its own specialized equipment including: a bath tub with shower; a bath bench; a functioning refrigerator and stove; stackable cones; a variety of hand dexterity apparatus; and a sewing machine. Appropriate supplies include: adapted eating utensils, dressing sticks, sock aids, button hooks, and reachers. The occupational therapy staff should consist of, at least one full-time occupational therapist, and a full-time occupational therapy assistant.

The speech therapy staff should consist of, at least a half-time speech-language pathologist, five days per week. The number of therapy patients in a true geriatric rehabilitation facility should be such, to require at least the above-mentioned staff.

In addition, the number of patients admitted to this facility under Medicare Part A insurance coverage should be very high. The number of residents discharged back to their homes outside the nursing home should also be high. This was one of the questions included on the list of interview questions for the PT during your tour so you already have this information available for your review. Another question on the list for the PT referred to home evaluations. A home evaluation should be completed just before every discharge. Therefore, the number of home evaluations performed by the PT and OT should be high and should approximate the number of discharges from this type of nursing home. An rare exception to this exists when the involved resident is being discharged to a location some distance away. An example

of this exception is Mrs. Eaton who was being discharged to live with her son in another state. Under
these circumstances, a home evaluation could not be
completed due to the excessive distance.

Another feature of a Geriatric Rehabilitation Facility
is that the number of residents being physically restrained will be very low or none at all. This is the result
of the skilled services of the PT and OT. Since these
professionals are in the facility full-time, they are better
able to address the needs of all of the residents, instead
of just those residents currently covered by Medicare
Part A insurance.

All Inclusive Retirement Community

This type of facility is a multi-level nursing home
meaning this nursing home cares for residents with
various handicaps and disabilities requiring fluctuating
amounts of assistance in their daily lives. The building is
divided into different sections depending upon the
amount of assistance required by the residents living
there. Likewise, anyone admitted to this type of nursing
home is assigned to the section in which they will
receive the necessary assistance. For example, Mr.
Cooper walks by himself but needs help getting in and
out of bed. He has severe diabetes so his diet and
medications need to be carefully monitored. Mr. Cooper
is admitted to the section of this nursing home in which
his diet will be closely monitored by a dietitian, his
medications will be carefully monitored by a licensed
nurse, and a CNA will be available to assist him in and
out of bed.

This facility includes three basic sections or levels.
One is a retirement setting for those residents who are
able to live on their own without assistance. The second

is an assisted living section for those residents who require only minimal assistance for more strenuous activities such as cooking and laundry. Last, there is a nursing home section for those residents requiring twenty-four-hour nursing care. In extremely large facilities, these different sections may be housed in separate buildings in a campus environment.

This multi-level arrangement is popular among large corporate-owned nursing homes and with corporations which own a number of smaller facilities in a relatively small geographic area. By offering various levels of care, residents tend to stay in this one setting as their health fluctuates instead of going to another facility to receive more intense medical care.

This sounds like an ideal situation, since you can move from one type of living arrangement to another as your health fluctuates. It is a tempting offer to have your home secure and all of your needs provided for the rest of your life. For example, Mrs. Grove is an 87 years old and recently widowed. She still lives in the home which her husband built 60 years ago and provides for herself very well. However, since her husband's death, she has felt isolated and lonely. A multi-level retirement community has just opened across town. Many of her friends have already moved in and she is tempted to join them. The advertisement she received in the mail shows several buildings surrounding a central beautifully landscaped courtyard. One building has independent apartments for people like herself who don't need any help but want companionship. Another building has apartments adapted for handicapped people or those needing some assistance with heavier chores and housekeeping. A third building has a small hospital of sorts for those people needing around-the-clock nursing care. The fourth building was listed on the brochure as an administration building and the whole community reminded her more of college campus than a retirement home. It looked very nice and it even said in the brochure that the residents could move from one building to another if they became ill. Why, she could just live there with her friends for the rest of her life. She didn't like the idea of selling her home. After all, she had lived here for all of her adult life and raised her children here. Still, the brochure looked very nice. She would have to think about this....

The security of this arrangement sounds too good to be true, and it is. The advertised only what the owner wanted Mrs. Grove to know and neglected to share the information that Mrs. Groves needs to know. Seaside Estates is a factual example of a retirement community which is housed in one large building, including a skilled nursing section, assisted living apartments, and retirement apartments. The residents who "buy in" to this building pay a one time fee of $65,000. Most of these residents sell their homes to raise this money. Each resident is then billed a monthly room rate of $100.00 for the remainder of their lives. This monthly charge includes room and board plus all of their medical care. However, this arrangement puts the corporation in the position of life-time landlord and the resident is a captive tenant. If the resident wanted to leave, she might feel that she could not, since her home had already been sold and such a large sum of money had been invested in the nursing home. She has no other home. In addition, if a resident felt abused or neglected by a member of the staff, they may feel that they cannot report it since they rely upon these individuals for their care.

What if the retirement went out of business? Nursing homes go out of business everyday and in this situation, all of these residents are likely to lose their investment and their housing. These residents have no place to go since they already sold their homes to make the initial "buy-in". Therefore, the security of a lifetime "buy-in" arrangement is not that secure.

The allure of an all-inclusive Retirement Community is understandable, and the concept is a good one: Several buildings or sections of a building in which the residents can receive varying amounts of assistance all in one location. Expand this idea by allowing the residents to move from one building to another as their health fluctuates, thus providing for their health for the remainder of their lives. This is as excellent idea! However, the resident should not be forced to make a sizable down payment just to gain entrance into this community. There should be no "buy in" of any kind. The resident should not be held as a captive tenant hesitant to report incidents of abuse for fear of retaliation from the same caregivers who committed the abuse in the first place. Removal of the "buy-in" would free the resident from these financial ties and would remove this power of the life-time corporate landlord.

Standard Nursing Home

The **Standard Nursing Home** differs from all three of the previously mentioned facilities in that there is little or no marketing of their services. Due to a variety of contributing factors they have nothing to advertise. The PT and OT are on the premises for only two or three hours a day, five days a week or less. The speech-language pathologist is seldom in the building, only when requested by the nursing staff. The Restorative

Nursing Care Program is a mere shadow of what it should be and exists only to satisfy the state regulation that the nursing home must have such a program. The therapy department, if one exists at all, is small with little or no useful equipment.

The standard nursing home has few admissions of residents covered by Medicare Part A insurance. There are no discharges of residents out of the nursing home back to their own homes in the community. The only residents that are discharged are those who have died. This type of facility provides maintenance care for its residents, to make them comfortable for the remainder of their lives. The physical needs of residents are the only concern of the staff and even these basic needs are seldom met.

The most obvious indicator of the poor care is the stench. Everywhere is the foul odor of urine on the residents, on the furniture, on the floors. It seems to permeate the entire building.

The other indicator is the residents themselves. They are fed, but the meals are bland and tasteless. They remain in the same clothes, usually pajamas, for several days until bath day. Their hair has not been combed. Their glasses stay on the dresser or in a drawer so they cannot see clearly. The men have not been shaven in days and when they have been shaved their faces bear the cuts of a careless, dull razor. Their hands are soiled with a disgusting filth consisting of food, human waste, and other unidentifiably substances. These residents sit in their wheelchairs or lie in bed all day, doing nothing. They do nothing but wait. They wait to die.... This is the basis for the term "warehousing the elderly" since that is essentially the purpose of the standard nursing home.

Chapter Summary

Transitional Care Facilities advertise a complete spectrum of services and emphasize an average length of stay of 20 days or less. These facilities discharge residents within 20 days regardless of their recovery status. Since most residents require more than 20 days to recover, they are discharged to yet another nursing home.

Geriatric Rehabilitation Facilities advertise their Medicare certified section with physical, occupational, and speech therapy services. Each department is fully equipped and staffed. This facility has a high rate of Medicare admissions and a high rate of discharges of residents back to their homes outside the building. The number of home evaluations is very high since one is completed just prior to each discharge and the number of physical restraints in the building is very low due to the timely intervention of the rehab professionals.

The All Inclusive Retirement Community is a multi-level facility which houses residents of various handicaps and disabilities requiring fluctuating amounts of assistance. This arrangement allows easy access to different living arrangements and services as ones health needs change but it comes at an exorbitant price. A staggering buy-in fee requires most prospective residents to sell their homes and this is followed by a monthly room and board fee. Once ensconced, the resident is unable to leave since their have no other home and have made a considerable investment in this facility. If the building goes out of business or is sold to another owner, the residents will find themselves cast out in the street with no home and no money.

The Standard Nursing Home does not advertise since they have nothing to advertise. If any rehab professionals visit, their visits are very short. There are few Medicare admissions and the only reason for discharge is death. The stench of urine and the filthy residents are reliable indicators of the poor quality of care in this type of facility.

Chapter 8
Legal Protection

I n this chapter, you will learn how to conduct background checks verifying business and professional licenses. The **Long Term Care Ombudsman** is given particular emphasis as a source of reliable information and for addressing your concerns. You will also learn the basic rights retained by each nursing home resident and the responsibilities of that resident or their family to the nursing home.

Background Checks

Substantial progress has been made in your search for a nursing home. The majority of nursing homes from your original list have been eliminated leaving only one or two candidates for further scrutiny. This will involve the legal protection of a background check to verify that this nursing home is operating within the law.

The first step is to call the state licensing board for nursing homes. All nursing homes are licensed by the state in which they are located, so the telephone number should be listed under state government in your local telephone book. Verify that this nursing home is licensed, that their license is current, and that there are no unresolved complaints filed against it. In addition, call the Better Business Bureau in your city. This telephone number is also listed in your local telephone book.

Verify that there are no unresolved complaints filed against this nursing home with this agency.

The next step involves the **Long-Term Care Ombudsman** in your area. Federal law requires each State agency on aging to establish an **Office of the Long-Term Care Ombudsman**. These offices can provide assistance and information to older Americans, their families and friends regarding nursing homes. The Long Term Care Ombudsman receives and investigates complaints made by or on behalf of nursing home residents and works to resolve the problems. Any serious violations are referred to the State Health Department. The Long-Term Care Ombudsman is listed in your local telephone book in the government pages. Inquire about any complaints against the nursing home. Ask for the number of complaints filed against this nursing home, the nature of those complaints, and the results and conclusions of the investigation into these complaints. If there are any serious, unresolved complaints against this nursing home, mark it off your list and move on.

There are a small number of professional background checks to be completed including the administrator, physical therapist, and attending physician. All nursing home administrators are licensed by the state in which they practice. The telephone number for the state licensing board for administrators is listed under state government in your local telephone book. Verify that this administrator's license is current with no unresolved complaints filed against it.

All physical therapists are licensed by the state in which they practice. The telephone number for the state licensing board for physical therapy is also listed under state government in your local telephone book. Verify that the physical therapist's license is current with no unresolved complaints filed against it.

The last professional background check involves the physician who will care for your loved one in the nursing home. If their regular doctor will not be taking care of them in the nursing home, find out the name(s) of all of the doctors who provide care at this nursing home, giving particular attention to the doctor designated at the medical director.

All medical doctors are licensed by the state in which they practice, so the telephone number of the state licensing board for physicians is listed under state government in your local telephone book. Verify that each physician's license is current with no unresolved complaints filed against it.

Basic Rights

All residents are entitled to the same rights inside the nursing home as they have when living outside of the nursing home. This is the case regardless of their current physical or mental status. For instance, they have the right to accept or refuse medications or medical treatment; No staff member can force them to take their medications or see their doctor. They have the right to eat or skip a meal; No one can force them to eat or drink if they don't want too.

As a nursing home resident, your relative has all of these rights regardless of physical or mental status unless a **Legal Guardian** is designated. The issue of "Legal Guardianship" is a judicial matter for which your attorney should be consulted.

When a senior citizen enters a nursing home, one of the most important legal rights retained is the right to their own medical records. The information stored in their medical chart is their personal property. You or your loved one have the right to review this information at anytime. You also are entitled to have the chart reviewed by an independent medical reviewer. The nursing home is required by law to give it to you, but be prepared to pay a nominal copying fee.

This right to review the medical chart is considered one of the most important legal rights because this document provides evidence of the quality of medical care received in the nursing home. This evidence may be useful if there is any suspicion of neglect or abuse toward your loved one. Of course, we all hope that our loved one would never be the victim of abuse or neglect at the hands of anyone responsible for their care, but this happens more often than we like to believe. Many unpleasant situations may ultimately end up in either criminal or civil court, involving abuse and neglect of the elderly as well as violation of their rights to proper care. Juries are also becoming more aware of this problem and are awarding large amounts in both punitive and compensatory damages. Therefore, if there is any suspicion of wrongdoing by the nursing home staff, exercise your right to review the chart.

Although your loved one retains all of their rights when they are admitted to a nursing home, they do not retain all of their responsibilities. One of those involves paying the bill. Any portion of the bill not covered by insurance will be passed along to the family member or friend who is designated in the medical chart as the **responsible party**.

This designation is found just inside the front or back cover of the resident's chart on an identification sheet. This sheet includes all of the demographic information regarding the resident, such as name, address, telephone number, emergency contact, religious affiliation, attending physician and telephone number, hospital of choice, mortuary of choice, and responsible party. All of these categories are self-explanatory except for "responsible party". This refers to the person responsible for paying the bill in the event that the resident is unable to pay. The responsible party has no legal decision-making authority, unlike a Power of Attorney or Legal Guardian. They are merely a financially responsible contact, usually a family member. However, if the resident has a designated Power of Attorney or Legal Guardian, then that person is also the responsible party. Whomever is listed in this blank on the identification sheet is the one who should be contacted when a change in medication is ordered by the attending physician or when a fall occurs.

Chapter Summary

A background check of the nursing home involves a telephone call to the state licensing board for nursing homes to verify that it is licensed to operate and that their license is current with no unresolved complaints filed against it. The Better Business Bureau is another source to check for complaints. A telephone call to the Long Term Care Ombudsman will reveal if there are any complaints filed with the federal government against this nursing home, the nature of those complaints, and the outcome of any investigations.

Professional background checks include the administrator, physical therapist, and attending physician. The licenses of each of these health professionals can be verified by telephone calls to their respective state licensing boards.

All nursing home residents are entitled to the same rights inside the facility as they enjoyed when living in their own home. They have the right to take their medication or skip a dose; eat or skip a meal; see their doctor or refuse his attentions. Each nursing home resident retains all of these rights regardless of their physical or mental condition unless a Legal Guardian is legally arranged.

The right to review their own medical record is one of the most important legal rights retained by the nursing home resident. The resident's family member also has the right to review this document or have it reviewed by a professional medical reviewer. Since this document provides evidence of the quality of care received by the resident in the nursing home, it is of great importance in the event of possible abuse or neglect.

The individual designated as the responsible party of the identification sheet in the resident's chart will be billed for any charges not covered by the resident's insurance carrier. This designation is merely a financial contact for the benefit of the nursing home and has no actual decision-making authority for the care of the resident unless they are also hold legal Power Of Attorney for that resident's affairs. The issues of Legal Guardianship and Power Of Attorney are judicial matters which are best discussed with your attorney.

Chapter 9
Medical Director

This chapter focuses on the medical director as the resident's attending physician. You will learn the most common reason for the medical director to attend to the majority of many nursing home residents. A list of interview questions is provided followed by a detailed explanation of each. Factual examples are used to further illustrate pertinent points.

Attending Physician

The most vital contributor to maintaining the health and vitality of your loved ones is their attending physician. In an ideal situation, their regular doctor would continue to attend to them in the nursing home but this situation is rare. The most common reason for an attending physician to refuse to care for a patient when they are admitted to a nursing home is that the reimbursement rate is lower for nursing home residents than for outpatients who come to their office.

Ask your loved one's regular doctor if s/he will continue to care for them while they are in the nursing home. If s/he declines, it will be necessary to ask the nursing home administrator to arrange a meeting with the visiting physician who will be caring for them. The majority of residents in any facility are attended by the nursing home's **Medical Director**. However, this physician typically does not have an office at the nursing home so they cannot be interviewed as a part of your scheduled tour.

Interview Questions

The following is a list of questions for the Medical Director to determine the quality of care s/he provides to the nursing home residents. These questions will also reveal if s/he spends adequate time caring for each resident.

1. How many patients do you have at this nursing home?
2. How often do you come to this nursing home?
3. How many patients are seen at each visit?
4. Approximately how much time do you spend with each patient?
5. Do you have an office or clinic to see outpatients?
6. Do you take care of patients at any other nursing home?
7. How many patients do you see at those other nursing homes?
8. Do you serve as Medical Director at any other nursing home?
9. Who reimburses you for the patients seen at the nursing home?
10. How much are you reimbursed for those visits?
11. How much would you charge my loved one under their insurance?

These questions will reveal the information necessary to make an informed decision about this nursing home's medical director. You will gain information regarding this physician's methods of practicing medicine and how frequently s/he attends to their more-vulnerable patients. From these answers, you will be able determine if you want your loved one to be one of their patients.

1. How many patients do you have at this nursing home?

Since the medical director typically attends to the majority of the nursing home's residents, expect this number to be remarkably high. It may encompass the facility's entire population.

The medical director frequently attends to as many residents as possible. By seeing a large number of residents during each weekly visit, he makes the trip financially worthwhile since he is reimbursed on a per-patient basis. However, this raises the question of the question: *How much time is spent with each resident?* and *Can an adequate examination be performed on each resident under this time constraint?* These questions will be addressed later in this chapter.

2. How often do you come to this nursing home?

3. How many patients are seen at each visit?

State regulations mandate that each nursing home resident must be seen by his or her attending physician at least once each month. In order to comply with these regulations, the medical director will visit the nursing home one day a week seeing a fraction of the residents at each visit. By the end of the month, however, s/he has seen all of the residents thereby complying with this regulation.

4. Approximately how much time do you spend with each patient?

The doctor will probably give a vague answer such as it depends upon the condition of the patient. However, an estimate of the time spent with each resident is necessary. This will determine if the doctor is able to devote an adequate amount of time to each patient examination or if they are over-worked with no possibility of keeping up with the demand for their services.

This answer will also determine if the doctor is charging for services he has not provided. For example, Dr. Lamb was the medical director of five distinct nursing homes (one for each day of the week) and was the attending physician of 80% of the residents in each facility. He visited each of these nursing homes weekly and always came on the same day. He arrived promptly at 8:00am, saw 36 residents and left promptly at 12:00 noon for his afternoon golf game. This calculates to 9 residents per hour. How is this possible?

His illegal method of practice made it possible. He required the charge nurse to give him a verbal report on the condition of each resident, while he stood outside the residents room and peeked through the open door. He then wrote an entry into the medical chart and signed it as his own. He moved swiftly down the hall with the charge nurse at his side and never entered a resident's room.

5. Do you have an office or clinic to see outpatients?

All nursing home medical directors should have an outpatient clinic. Even a doctor specializing in **geriatrics**, should have an outpatient clinic to see senior citizens who live in the community at large. If this physician's entire practice consists solely of nursing home residents, then this situation raises suspicions regarding their medical practice. Mark this physician and this nursing home off your list and move on.

6. Do you take care of patients at any other nursing home?

7. How many patients do you see at those other nursing homes?

The medical director of one facility will often have patients in other nursing homes even if they are not the medical director of those buildings. One doctor can not properly care for so many complicated patients. Since the typical nursing home resident has numerous medical problems each with its own set of complications, medications, and side-effects, one doctor can not possibly spend an adequate amount of time examining each individual. Therefore, they don't. The care by the physician is substandard or, as evidenced by the example of Dr. Lamb, is nonexistent.

8. Do you serve as Medical Director at any other nursing home?

The common practice of serving as medical director at more than one nursing home takes on added dimension with the administrative duties of this role. These added duties make the doctor's time even more valuable.

In addition to providing care to the majority of residents at each of these nursing homes, s/he has the responsibilities of the office of medical director. These duties include numerous meetings such as Utilization Review, Quality Assurance, and Board of Directors meetings.

Utilization Review is a monthly meeting in which the nursing homes methods for administering Medicare benefits are reviewed and discussed, such as who receives them and why. Quality Assurance is a monthly meeting in which the care received by the residents is discussed as well as how many falls occurred that month and why. The Board of Directors meetings usually occur quarterly and address the financial operation of the nursing home. These are meetings for discussing all aspects of the nursing home operation and corporate business and are attended only by the high ranking personnel.

It is impossible for one doctor to attend all of these meetings at more than one facility and still have time to see the majority of the residents in each building. There is simply not enough hours in the day.

9. Who reimburses you for the patients seen at the nursing home?
10. How much are you reimbursed for those visits?

The answers to these questions will reveal any financial incentive for this physician to serve as medical director for as many nursing homes as possible, and to attend to as many patients as possible. Do not be dissuaded if the doctor hesitates to answer. Remember, this should be public information and a part of the nursing home business/accounting information.

In some states, a physician is reimbursed approximately $17 per patient-visit in a nursing home. This falls far short of the regular $35 to $50 per visit which the doctor could charge for an office call for out-patients like you and me.

The financial incentive is firmly in place for a doctor to refuse to attend to nursing home residents, or to attend to a very large number of residents at each nursing home visit to make their time at the facility more profitable.

In addition, serving as a nursing home's medical director is one method of securing the majority of the facility's residents as their own patients, and thus increasing the profitability of each visit to the nursing home.

11. How much would you charge my loved one under their insurance?

This answer will obviously reveal the precise charge for this doctor to visit your loved one in the nursing home. This will also inform you if this doctor charges different rates depending upon the patients ability to pay or depending upon the extent of insurance coverage available.

Chapter Summary

The attending physician is the most vital contributor to the health of a nursing home resident. An individual's regular doctor will typically refuse to continue caring for them after their admission to a nursing home since the insurance reimbursement rate for nursing home residents is low.

The majority of residents in any nursing home are attended by that facility's medical director. A list of interview questions for the medical director was provided in this chapter and explained in detail. The factual example of Dr. Lamb further illustrated the common illegal practice of some medical directors.

Chapter 10
Restraints

I n this chapter, you will learn the legal definition of a physical and **chemical restraint** as mandated by the OBRA regulations. You will learn the proper uses for restraints and the common methods in which they are being misused in nursing homes today. Particular attention is given to the identification of the type of resident at risk for abuse through the use of restraints.

Common Occurrence

It may seem inconceivable that your loved one may some day be tied down against their will to their bed or a wheelchair. As difficult and heart-wrenching as this is to think about, it is a probability for which you must be prepared. One day in the near future when you walk into the nursing home to visit your loved one, you will find them tied down to their bed or wheelchair, pulling against the restraints, trying with all of their strength to break free. This atrocity can happen in any nursing home, even in those "good" nursing homes with plush, expensive furnishings and immaculately groomed lawns.

What is a Restraint?

The OBRA '87 regulations define a restraint as any device which restricts or impedes the resident's movement in any way and which the resident cannot remove without assistance. These regulations recognize two basic categories of restraints, mechanical or **physical restraints** and **chemical restraints**.

Physical restraints

Traditionally, a category of physical restraints included tie-down vests, waist restraints, mitts, wrist straps and ankle straps. However, the OBRA definition broadened the scope of this list to include geri-chairs, gates, lap-trays which fasten in the back of the wheelchair and any other device which the resident cannot unfasten or remove by himself.

According to OBRA's definition, there are many ways to restrain a resident without tying them down. If your relative is lying in bed and cannot change their position or get out of bed, then they are restrained. A more detailed example of this is illustrated by Mrs. Jones who is lying on her side in bed, with a large pillow behind their back to prevent them from rolling over, and the bed rails up on both sides of the bed.

Side-lying with a pillow behind their back is the most common position in which nursing home residents are placed when in bed and it is the preferred positioning technique taught in the CNA training courses. However, according to the OBRA definition, it is a form of restraint. Very few nursing home residents could remove the pillow, and no resident could lower their own bed rail. With both bed rails up, they are prevented from getting out of bed by themselves and with a large pillow behind their back which they cannot remove, they are prevented from rolling onto their back.

Mr. Hill provides an example of a nontraditional wheelchair restraint. He is seated in a wheelchair with a lap-tray placed on the armrests. This lap-tray is secured with two straps tied in a knot at the back of the chair and out of his reach. He strains unsuccessfully to remove the tray but the unrelenting knot holds him captive in the chair. Although a lap-tray does not have the usual appearance of a restraint tying a resident down, it restricts his movement and he cannot remove it without assistance. Therefore, by the OBRA definition, this lap-tray is a physical restraint.

At first glance, Mr. Hill and Mrs. Jones may not appear to be restrained since their hands and feet are free of bindings. However, according to OBRA '87, they are. These two examples are used to illustrate that the term restraint is no longer limited to bindings which visibly tie the resident down. Restraints can take on a variety of forms.

Chemical Restraints

The second category of restraint recognized by OBRA is chemical restraints which consists of medications and drugs whose purpose is to alter the resident's state of mind. This category includes such drugs as Lithium, Mellaril, and Haldol, among others. The stronger chemical restraints are referred to in the medical chart as psychotropic drugs, and are prescribed by the doctor for residents who exhibit abusive or aggressive behaviors.

The use of these drugs should be strictly regulated since they are addictive and have severe side effects. However, the charge nurse frequently elects to administer one or more of these drugs on a "trial" basis without a consultation or prescription from the attending physician. She commits this illegal act when a resident shows anti-social or undesirable behavior, especially at night when she does not want to be bothered. The resident is unable to advocate for their own rights and there are no residual effects visible the next morning so this crime is rarely reported.

Residents At Risk

Restraints, both physical and chemical are most often applied to residents who are at risk of falling, tend to wander, or become agitated during a nursing procedure. However, even in instances involving these three types of residents, a restraint is not necessary if the situation is managed properly, in a professional manner.

Frequent Falls

The first type of resident at risk for restraints is one who fall daily or several times each day. In their attempt to protect the resident or relieve themselves of the frustration, will apply a restraint thinking that if the resident cannot get up, they cannot fall. In reality, applying a restraint has the opposite effect. The restrained resident will become agitated and strain even harder to get up, sometimes to the point of causing injury to himself.

A resident who is at risk for falling should not be restrained, they should be referred to physical therapy for evaluation so the reason for their falls can be investigated and resolved.

Wandering

The second type of resident at risk for restraints is the one who tends to wander. The nursing home staff will document in the resident's chart any one of a variety of reasons to justify the restraint. Among those reasons most commonly documented are:

1. For the resident's safety.

2. So the resident does not wander off the premises.
3. So the resident does not go outside during in-
   clement weather.
4. To prevent the resident from wandering into
   other residents' rooms.

The administration and staff of many nursing homes consider these to be acceptable reasons for restraining the wandering resident, but they are not. They are just excuses to explain away what is really happening.

OBRA regulations mandate that the nursing home administrator and owners are responsible for keeping the building and grounds safe for all of the residents and to admit only those residents who can function safely in that environment. If this home is not safe for the resident to wander freely, the administrator should not admit him. However if the census is low, s/he will admit all of the residents he can, just to keep the beds full.

This problem is compounded when the staff restrains residents like Mrs. Bertram to prevent her from wander-ing. Her chart reads that the she was restrained for her own safety. However if this building is not a safe environment for her to wander freely, then she should not have been admitted. If her wandering tendencies began after her admission, then is the responsibility of the administrator to transfer her to a facility which is equipped to care for her.

Mrs. Bertram could also restrained for the conve-nience of the staff, so they do not have to constantly watch her as she wanders in the building.

Agitation
The third type of resident who is frequently restrain-ed is the one who becomes agitated during a medical

procedure. The nursing home staff believes that this is one instance in which a restraint is always necessary. However, the use of a restraint is not necessary if the health professionals handles the situation properly and with sensitivity.

The most common reason for a resident to become agitated is out of fear of what is happening to him or from rough handling so if the health professional avoids frightening the resident, a restraint is not necessary.

Proper Procedure

Although most situations do not warrant the use of a restraint if the decision is made that one is necessary, a prescription must be signed by the attending physician for the type of restraint and for its specific use. There can be no "standing" orders for a "restraint as needed". Restraints cannot be used at the discretion of the staff for their convenience or to punish the resident for some undesirable behavior.

Regardless of these laws, in many facilities such bonds are applied by the staff without a physician's prescription. In some cases, they are applied by the CNA with no documentation at all. If it is documented, it is recorded as a "trial" usage. However this indiscriminate application violates state and federal regulations and the resident's rights. When a restraint is considered necessary, the following detailed procedure, or a similar procedure must be followed prior to the application of that device:

1. The problem must be documented by the charge nurse.

2. The PT or OT must evaluate the resident for a functional status change and document the results.
3. The resident's family or responsible party must be consulted and this consultation must be documented.
4. The attending physician must sign a prescription for the least restrictive, safest device.
5. The restraint must be applied according to the proper manufacturer's instructions.
6. All appropriate family and staff members must be trained in the application and removal of the restraint.
7. The restraint must be checked frequently for causing **edema**, **abrasions**, or **pallor** of the arm or leg.
8. The care team should re-evaluate the need for the restraint at least quarterly.
9. The restraint should be removed as soon as the resident's condition permits.

This procedure or one similar to this, should be in place in every nursing home in this country. However, if the nursing home has a formal written policy similar to the one outlined here, it is rarely followed. Restraints are applied by CNAs with no training in their application and with no documentation on the medical charts.

Long-time residents are seldom evaluated by a PT or OT for changes in their health or condition. If a restraint evaluation is completed at all, it is performed by a less qualified staff member, such as a PTA or RNA. Family members are rarely consulted. The resident is left without monitoring for the majority of the day until that resident is put back to bed, either after lunch or at bedtime. Finally, since the current residents are not re-evaluated regularly, they are overlooked for less restrictive devices or for complete removal of the restraint. In short, once a resident is restrained, they remain that way.

Chapter Summary

OBRA regulations define a restraint as any device which restricts the resident's movements in any way and which the resident cannot remove without assistance.

Traditionally, a physical restraint actually tied a resident to their bed or wheelchair but the OBRA regulations have broadened this category to include such items as pillows and lap-trays if they impede the residents movements.

Chemical restraints are drugs used to alter the residents' state of mind. These drugs are just as effective as physical restraints at restricting a resident's movements but there are no visible bonds. These drugs are frequently referred to as psychotropic medications and must be prescribed by a physician. Since these drugs are addictive and have severe side effects, they should be strictly regulated but in the late night hours the charge nurse frequently administers them for her own convenience to keep the residents quiet.

Residents who fall frequently are at risk for being restrained since it is more convenient for the nurses to tie them down rather than initiate the proper evaluation procedure with the rehab staff. Wandering residents are frequently restrained so the nursing staff does not have to watch them. If a wandering resident's chart reflects that the reason for the restraint is for the resident's safety, then this building is not a safe environment for this resident and they should be discharged to a nursing home which can provide a safe environment. If a resident becomes agitated from rough handling or fearful of the unknown during a medical procedure, they will be restrained.

Situations which require the use of a restraint are rare but when they occur, the proper steps must be taken to protect the rights and health of the resident. The nursing homes which possess a written restraint policy rarely use it. It is more common for the nurses and CNAs to indiscriminately apply these devices for their own convenience.

Chapter 11:
Financial Incentives

This chapter focuses on the methods used by the administrators and corporate owners manipulate their employees into violating laws and regulations in an effort to cut their operating costs. You will learn the ramifications of these acts upon the individual staff member if they submit to this coercion. Particular attention is given to legal ramifications.

Manipulation

There is considerable financial incentive for the nursing home administrators and corporate owners to "cut corners" in the quality of care for the residents. These measures are difficult to trace since various staff members are used to carry out the illegal acts. An example of this cost cutting occurs when the administrator directs the PT to discharge a Medicare Part A patient from skilled physical therapy services on day 101 when their Medicare coverage runs out, regardless of the resident's need for more therapy.

Unfortunately, even though the administrator has pressured the PT to discharge the resident early, the therapist is professionally responsible for this action and her license hangs is at risk. This places the PT in a difficult situation.

If this patient is discharged from skilled physical therapy services when their Medicare Part A coverage is exhausted on day 101, there are issues of **abandonment**

of care for the PT who was treating this patient. If the resident still needs therapy, the PT cannot stop treating them just because the insurance company stops paying for it. If she does, she may be guilty of abandoning this patient. Furthermore, if injury occurs as a result of this premature discharge, malpractice may also be an issue.

Malpractice

This legal term is defined by civil law rather than criminal law. By civil definition, malpractice is negligence which occurs in the performance of professional duties. Therefore, if the PT surrenders to the pressure from the administrator--who is also her supervisor--to discharge the resident on day 101 regardless of the resident's health, that PT may be guilty of malpractice.

Regardless of this professional harassment, the responsibility for any injury to the resident is placed upon the PT rather than the administrator. This occurs because the therapist is the professional who discharged the resident from services and her signature is on the discharge forms. In addition, any coercion from the administrator is usually verbal so it is the word of the administrator against the word of the therapist.

Breach of Contract

In addition to malpractice, there is also the issue of a contract for service between the physical therapist and the resident. The relationship between the PT and the resident can be described as an implied contract. The contract is entered into, when the PT accepts the patient and the patient knowingly seeks the therapy services.

This therapist-patient relationship encompasses the trust of the patient in the PT. This relationship also imposes a **fiduciary** duty upon the therapist as well as demanding loyalty and an avoidance of conflict of interest. Therefore, the PT has a duty to act in the resident's best interests.

In contrast to her professional ethics and legal responsibilities to the residents, the staff PT is bound by the administrator to act in the best financial interest of the nursing home which is rarely in the best interest of the resident's health. In this situation, the physical therapist's job is threatened if they did not comply with their administrator's demands to treat the residents based on their finances rather than on their functional needs.

In some of these instances, the PT will terminate their employment rather than violate their professional ethics and licensure regulations. It the misfortune of the residents and the nursing home industry that the majority of these PTs also leave geriatrics in search of a higher standard of practice.

As mentioned previously, if the therapist chooses to discharge the patient due to a lack of insurance coverage, even though further treatment is indicated, the therapist may be at risk for claims based on abandonment of care. However, if a doctor discontinues therapy, that action creates liability for the doctor. In this case, the definition of the doctor-therapist relationship protects the therapist since the therapist must treat the resident according to the doctor's prescription.

Insurance Denial

The insurance carrier is a source of professional conflict which will become more prevalent with the growth of managed care. This conflict occurs when the doctor orders continued physical therapy treatment and the managed care payer denies further payment. The physical therapist is responsible for following the doctor's order and continuing care even though the facility is not paid for it. If the administrator directs the therapist to discharge the patient because the insurance company is not paying for the treatment, the therapist is in a "Catch-22". If she obeys the doctor's order, she could lose her job. If she obeys the administrator, she is violating state and federal law, and could lose her license. Either way, the therapist is held responsible since her signature is on the treatment forms. The administrator is not held responsible for promoting illegal behavior, since it is his word against the therapist's.

The PT may appeal the decision of the managed care payer using whatever appeal process this payer has established. In addition, an appeal at this point is considered to be a part of the therapist's duty to the patient. However, the administrator will not support this since the treatments will continue during the appeal process with a probable result of nonpayment for the original treatments and for the treatments occurring during the appeal process.

The last option left to the PT is to continue treating the resident at their expense. However, if this last option is chosen, the resident, their family, and responsible party must be properly consulted or they are within their rights to refuse payment.

Fraudulent Billing

A common financial incentive for the administrator concerns the interaction of the skilled physical therapist and the restorative nursing care program. From an accounting standpoint, this program is part of the general care of the resident and cannot be billed to Medicare Part A or B. However, skilled physical therapy services are billable. Therefore, many administrators include the services of the RNAs in the skilled physical therapy billing forms to Medicare. This is Medicare fraud and is illegal. In addition, if the nursing home uses the US Postal Service, this crime becomes mail fraud which is a felony.

These final billing forms are compiled by the administrator or his billing staff from information obtained from the billing sheets from physical therapy, occupational therapy, speech therapy, and nursing departments. Since no signature is required on these final Medicare billing sheets, the administrator and his entire billing staff can claim ignorance.

The PT, OT, and SLP have no part in the preparation of the Medicare billing forms but their signatures appear on their respective billing forms which are submitted to the business so the ruthless administrator will implicate one of these unsuspecting professionals if an investigation insues. Each of these innocent individuals is quickly cleared of any wrong-doing since it is easily proven that they complete only the billing form for their own discipline yet the experience of such an investigation has driven more than a few highly skilled therapists out of geriatrics.

Fraudulent billing can also occur in the individual therapy discipline when the administrator attempts to coerce the therapist into billing restorative nursing programs as if they were skilled therapy. If the therapist submits to this coercion, she is guilty of insurance fraud. If she refuses, she will lose her job.

Keep Them Ill

The most disgusting financial incentive for the administrator occurs in their method of reimbursement.

Nursing homes are reimbursed for the cost of caring for the residents based upon a **Case Mix Reimbursement System**. In simple terms, this means that the nursing home is paid more money for more debilitated residents and less money for those residents who are less debilitated. Therefore, if the resident's condition improves, the nursing home is paid less. Clearly, the financial incentive is in place to keep residents debilitated and most nursing homes due a very good job of doing just that.

Chapter Summary

Various staff members are manipulated by the administrator and corporate owners to carry out illegal acts. The PT is targeted for coercion into discharging residents as soon as their Medicare coverage expires regardless of their need for continued treatments. If she submits to this coercion, she may be guilty of abandoning this patient. If the resident sustains an injury as a result of this premature discharge, the PT may also be guilty of malpractice.

By civil definition, malpractice is negligence which occurs in the performance of professional duties. Regardless of the professional harassment from the administrator, the PT is responsible for any injury sustained by the resident as a result of premature discharge since her signature appears on the discharge form.

By discharging a resident prematurely, the PT has also breached the implied service contract which exists between a therapist and her patient. However, the staff PT is bound by her administrator to act in the best financial of the nursing home with complete disregard for the health of the residents, her professional responsibilities and legal ramifications.

If the insurance carrier refuses to pay for additional therapy but the doctor orders it, the therapist is bound by law to carry out the ordered treatments. The administrator will direct her to discontinue services for insurance denial and will even threaten her job if she refuses.

A common financial incentive for the administrator is to bill restorative nursing services to Medicare as if they were skilled therapy. This is insurance fraud and possibly mail fraud if the US Postal Service was used. The ruthless administrator will attempt to frame the individual therapists for this crime but they are quickly cleared of any wrong-doing since only contribution to the Medicare billing is the service log from their specific departments. Since no signature is required on the final Medicare billing forms, the administrator and his billing office staff can claim ignorance.

The most disgusting financial incentive occurs with the Case Mix Reimbursement System in which the amount of money which the nursing home is reimbursed is based on the state of debilitation of the residents. The sicker the resident, the more money the nursing home is paid. This is a clear incentive for the nursing home to keep their residents ill.

Conclusion

At some point in our lives, each of us will be faced with the very difficult and heart-wrenching dilemma of admitting a loved one to a nursing home. This task is never an easy one but you now have an understanding of how to choose a nursing home that will meet your needs. Armed with the information contained in the preceding chapters, you are prepared to meet this challenge.

Within your arsenal of knowledge, you have a list of questions to ask each targeted staff member during your educated tour of the nursing home. You have an in-depth understanding of each of those questions and a working familiarity with the terminology used by the members of this industry. Your newly acquired understanding of Medicare regulations, OBRA guidelines and the State survey process will prove useful in discerning truth from misleading marketing strategies and fraudulent financial incentives. Rehabilitation services have weighed heavily in the content of this book since the billing procedures for these services to Medicare and other insurance carriers leaves them open to fraudulent practices.

In writing this book, it has been my goal to shed some light on this confusing world of the nursing home industry. I hope that I have succeeded in enlightening you so that you stand ready to make the decision on which nursing home to entrust with the health, the well-being, and the daily care of your loved one.

Appendix A
Questions for
Telephone Interview

Nursing Home:

1. Who owns the nursing home?
2. Is it privately owned or corporate owned?
3. Is the nursing home Medicare certified?
4. How many Medicare-certified beds do they have?
5. How many residents can they have living there?
6. How many residents do they have living there?
7. Is there a waiting list?
8. How many people are on staff?
9. How many of those staff members take care of the residents?
10. Is there a physical therapist on staff?
11. How many days per week is physical therapy provided?
12. How many days per week is occupational therapy provided?
13. How many days per week is speech therapy provided?
14. How many days per week is restorative nursing care provided?

Appendix B
Tour Questions

Nursing Home:

Tour Guide
1. How many residents live in this nursing home?
2. How many beds are in this nursing home?
3. How many employees are on staff?
4. How many staff members take care of the residents?
5. How many of your residents are on Medicare today?
6. How many Medicare certified beds are in this nursing home?
7. How many patients were discharged back to their homes, outside of the facility last month?
8. When does discharge planning begin?
9. How long have you worked here?
10. Is there a licensed physical therapist on staff?

Physical Therapist
1. How many patients are receiving physical therapy services under Medicare Part A insurance coverage?
2. How many patients are receiving physical therapy services under Medicare Part B insurance coverage?

3. How many patients are receiving physical therapy services under private insurance coverage?
4. How many patients are receiving physical therapy services under Medicaid?
5. Are you involved with the Restorative Nursing Care program?
6. If the answer to 5 is "Yes", what is your involvement with the Restorative Nursing Care program?
7. Do you perform home evaluations?
8. How long have you worked here?
9. Are you an employee or a contractor?
10. How many hours per day do you work here?
11. Do you work in this nursing home every day?

Restorative Nursing Aide
1. How long have you worked here?
2. What training have you had in order to perform this job?
3. How many hours per day do you work?
4. How many residents are you scheduled to work with, today?

Charge Nurse
1. How long have you worked here?
2. How many years of nursing school did you attend?
3. What was the topic of your most recent continuing education class and when was it held?
4. How often are the residents bathed? Can they be bathed more often if they wish?
5. At what times do the residents eat their meals?
6. How many residents in this nursing home are physically restrained?

7. How many residents in this nursing home are able to walk?
8. How many residents in this nursing home are in wheelchairs?
9. How many residents in this nursing home are bedbound?

Nurses' Aide
1. How long have you worked here?
2. What formal training qualifies you for this kind of work?
3. How many residents are in your care today?

Social Service Director
1. Will you assist with the admissions process?
2. Will you assist with Medicaid applications?
3. Are there established visiting hours?
4. Can the residents decorate their own room with personal belongings?
5. Does this nursing home have a residents' council?
6. Does the residents' council influence decisions concerning resident life?
7. Does the nursing home have a family council?
8. Does the family council influence decisions concerning resident life?
9. Are there private areas for residents to meet with their visitors or physician?

Administrator
1. How long have you worked here?
2. How much does Medicare reimburse the facility per resident?
3. How long does Medicare coverage last?

4. What is the room rate?
5. What services and supplies does this rate cover?
6. How much does Medicaid reimburse the facility per resident?
7. What services and supplies does this rate cover?
8. How long does Medicaid coverage last?
9. How many falls occurred in this building last month?
10. How many medical doctors come to this nursing home?
11. What other health professionals come to this nursing home?
12. How much does each of these services cost?
13. What precautions does the nursing home take to ensure the health of the residents during extreme weather?
14. What emergency provisions are stored here, in the event of a power outage?
15. Is the nursing home air-conditioned?
16. Are the residents allowed to smoke? Where?
17. Do you provide transportation to and from doctor's appointments?
18. Do you provide special services, such as ventilators and feeding tubes?
19. What is your policy regarding the purchase of prescription medications from our own pharmacist?
20. If my loved one requires hospitalization, to which hospital will they be sent?
21. Will their bed be available upon their return?
22. Is there a charge to hold the bed?
23. How much advance notice do you provide regarding an increase in the nursing home charges?

24. Does this nursing home accept special needs residents, such as Alzheimer's, or Aids?
25. Is the staff trained to care for these special residents?
26. Ask for references.

Appendix C
Interview Questions
for the Medical Director

Nursing Home:

1. How many patients do you have at this nursing home?
2. How often do you come to this nursing home?
3. How many patients are seen at each visit?
4. Approximately how much time do you spend with each patient?
5. Do you have an office or clinic to see outpatients?
6. Do you take care of patients at any other nursing home?
7. How many patients do you see at those other nursing homes?
8. Do you serve as Medical Director at any other nursing home?
9. Who reimburses you for the patients seen at the nursing home?
10. How much are you reimbursed for those visits?
11. How much would you charge my loved one under their insurance?

Glossary

Abandonment of Care: Refusal to care for or treat a resident without medical justification after that course of treatment has begun.

Abrasion: Scrape or scratch.

Administrator in Training: AIT. A student who is training to become a nursing home administrator.

AIT: *See* Administrator in Training

ALF: *See* Assisted Living Facility.

Allied Health Professionals: Members of the health profession other than the physicians and nurses. These individuals are typically outside the jurisdiction of the state survey process and include the physical therapist, occupational therapist, and dietitian, just to name a few.

Aspirate: The act of sucking foreign material into an airway, such as food or liquid.

Assisted Living Facility: ALF. A building in which the residents receive only minimal assistance with activities such as meal preparation, laundry and housekeeping.

Bachelor of Science degree in Nursing: BSN. A four year college degree in nursing. BSN also refers to the individual nurse with this degree.

Bath Aide: The Certified Nurses' Aide whose duty is to bath the residents.

Bed bound: The inability to get out of bed.

Bed Mobility: The ability to roll from side to side, change position and move around in bed.

BSN: *See* Bachelors of Science in Nursing.

Case Mix Reimbursement: A system in which a nursing home is reimbursed more money for more seriously ill and debilitated residents.

Census: The total number of residents in the nursing home.

Certified Nurses' Aide: CNA. An individual with a high school diploma or the equivalent who has completed nurses' aide training and passed a certification examination.

Change in Condition: The altered state of a residents health or abilities.

Chemical Restraint: A drug which restricts a resident's movements by altering their state of mind.

CNA: *See* Certified Nurses' Aide.

Cognition: The ability to think clearly and accurately.

Continuity of Care: The practice of having the same staff member perform the same treatment on the resident during each visit.

Contractor: A member of the nursing home staff who is employed by another company which signed a contract with this nursing home to provide services to their residents. Usually includes physical therapy, occupational therapy, and speech therapy.

Contracture: A permanent shortening of a muscle.

Coverage: The financial protection provided by an insurance company to pay health-related bills.

Date of Onset: The date at which the illness began or the injury occurred.

Direct Patient Care: The act of providing hands-on care to the residents.

Discharge Planner: The member of the hospital staff whose job it is to assist the family in making housing arrangements for their loved one in preparation for their discharge from the hospital.

Edema: Swelling.

Eligibility, eligible: Meeting the requirements for Medicare benefits for this illness or condition. For most people this occurs when they have been in the hospital for at least 3 days.

Endurance: The ability to continue a task.

Entitlement, entitled: Meeting the requirements for Medicare insurance coverage and to be enrolled in the Medicare program. For most people this occurs when they turn 65 years of age.

Exacerbation: A flare-up of an existing illness or condition.

F-tag: The numbering system used by the State survey team to identify each regulation. The F-tags listed in the survey report indicate the violated regulations.

Fiduciary: A service which is accepted because the resident and the public have faith in its value.

Function: The ability to perform a task.

Functional Independence: The ability to perform all aspects of daily care for oneself.

Functional Status: The resident's ability to move around and take care his personal needs.

Geri-chair: A padded reclining chair on wheels used for positioning residents for comfort as an alternative to being in bed all the time.

Geriatrics: The medical specialty of caring for and studying the conditions common to senior citizens. Pertaining to older adults over 65 years of age.

HCFA: *See* Health Care Financing Administration.

Health Care Financing Administration: The federal agency which governs the operation of nursing homes.

Home Evaluation: The examination of a resident's home and their ability to function in it.

Intermediary: An insurance company which has a contract with the Medicare Agency to administer Medicare benefits according to the regulations.

Legal Guardian: The individual who is invested by law with the total care of the resident and their estate.

Less Restrictive Support Device: Any device such as pillows or pads which provide security and personal safety to the resident without impeding their movements.

Level A Requirement: One of two distinctions used by the State surveyors to determine the quality of care in a nursing home. Level A refers to a consistent pattern of violations or a life threatening situation.

Level B Requirement: One of two distinctions used by the State surveyors to determine the quality of care in a nursing home. Level B refers to serious but infrequent, unrelated violations.

Licensed Practical Nurse: LPN. A nurse of either one or two years of training; This varies from state to state.

Long Term Care Ombudsman: Provides information to older Americans, their families and friends regarding nursing homes. Receives and investigates complaints made by or on behalf of nursing home residents.

LPN: *See* Licensed Practical Nurse.

Maintenance: The act of keeping a resident in the same condition.

Malpractice: Neglectful or illegal performance of duty especially when resulting in injury or loss of function.

Medical Director: The medical doctor who is responsible for the medical operation of the nursing home and attends to the majority of the residents.

Medicare Certified Bed: Each nursing home has a specific number of beds reserved for Medicare residents. A non-Medicare resident can occupy one of these bed but if a Medicare resident occupies a non-certified bed, Medicare will not pay for their care.

Medicare Certified: A nursing home which meets the criteria set by Medicare to participate in their program and is reimbursed by Medicare for the care of all residents meeting their qualifications.

Medicare Covered Day: A day during which all reasonable and customary expenses for a resident's care are covered by Medicare benefits.

Medicare Part A: Hospitalization insurance coverage for all individuals who meet the entitlement criteria. This is usually available to all senior citizens over 65 years of age.

Medicare Part B: Medical insurance coverage for those individuals who are enrolled in this insurance program and pay a monthly premium.

Mobility: The ability to move.

Nurse Practitioner: A nurse with a Masters degree in a specialty area of the nursing field. Rarely found in a nursing home.

Nurses' Aides: Those staff members who provide general personal care to the residents.

Nursing Home Candidate: A nursing home which is on your list of potential places for your loved one.

Occupational Therapist: OT. A health professional licensed in most states who evaluates and treats residents to improve their abilities to perform daily tasks such as dressing and grooming.

Occupational Therapy: A program of treatments whose goal is to improve a residents abilities to perform daily tasks such as dressing and grooming.

Optimum Level of Function: The stage at which a resident can progress no farther.

OT: *See* Occupational Therapist.

238 THE NURSING HOME CHOICE

Pallor: Whiteness of the skin in an area of the body.

Physical Restraint: Any tangible device which restricts the resident's movements.

Physical Therapist: PT. A licensed health professional who evaluates and treats residents to improve their abilities to live independently.

Physical Therapy Assistant: PTA. A therapy support person who is trained to carry out the resident's care plan as designed by the physical therapist.

Physical Therapy: A program of treatments whose goal is to improve a residents abilities to move around their home.

Physician's Order: Prescription.

Plan of Correction: A document written by the nursing home detailing their methods for resolving each of the violations cited by the survey team. Each resolution must describe the corrective action, identify the responsible staff members and explain any training necessary for its completion.

Posture-guard chair: A padded reclining chair on wheels with built-in adjustments for the residents specific needs.

Power of Attorney: The individual who has been given by the resident the legal ability to make financial and medical decisions for the resident.

PT: *See* Physical Therapist.

PTA: *See* Physical Therapy Assistant.

Reasonable and Customary: Those charges which the Medicare reviewer determines to be appropriate for payment.

Registered Nurse: RN. A nurse of two, three, or four years of training; This varies from state to state.

Rehab: Rehabilitation services including physical therapy, occupational therapy, and speech therapy.

Rehabilitation Services: The department whose goal is to improve the residents abilities to live as independently as possible, usually includes physical therapy, occupational therapy, and speech therapy.

Reimbursement Rate: The amount of money which the nursing home is paid by the insurance company for each resident whom qualifies for coverage.

Resident Outcome: The effect of an action upon the residents.

Resident-specific: Customized to the needs of that resident.

Responsible Party: The individual who is designated on the resident's identification to be accountable for the bills incurred in providing care to that resident.

Restorative Nursing Aide: RNA. A nurses' aide who performs maintenance exercises with the residents.

Restorative Nursing Care: A division of the nursing department whose goal is to maintain a resident's current abilities through exercise.

Restraint: Any device or drug which impedes a resident's movements and which the resident is unable to remove.

RN: *See* Registered Nurse.

RNA: *See* Restorative Nursing Aide.

Sixty Day Stay in the Spell of Illness: There must be 60 days since the last Medicare-covered day. A resident must be off of Medicare Part A for at least 60 days after the first illness in order to qualify for Medicare Part A benefits for the second illness.

Skilled Nursing Facility: SNF. A nursing home certified by the state government as providing 24 hour skilled nursing care.

SLP: *See* Speech/Language Pathologist.

SNF: *See* Skilled Nursing Facility.

Speech Therapist: SLP. A health professional who evaluates and treats residents to improve their ability to think clearly and communicate those thoughts. Also known as a speech/language pathologist.

Speech Therapy: A program of treatments whose goal is to improve a residents abilities to think clearly and communicate those thoughts.

Speech/Language Pathologist: SLP. A health professional who evaluates and treats residents to improve their ability to think clearly and communicate those thoughts. Also known as a speech therapist.

Spell of Illness: A specific time during which one was ill. There is a date on which the illness began and one of recovery.

Spend Down: A Medicaid requirement to liquidate your assets and spend the proceeds before receiving government assistance.

Staff to Resident Ratio: The number of staff members per every resident in the nursing home.

Standing Orders: Physician's orders regarding the care of the resident which remain on the chart from one month to the next. For example, Out of bed as desired; Out of building with family and friends as desired; Regular diet; Walks independently with walker.

State Survey: The process used by the State government and State Department of Health to examine the operation of nursing homes for violations of state and federal regulations in an effort to enforce those regulations.

Stop Placement: The official operational status imposed on a nursing home by the state survey team of being barred from admitting new residents until such time as current violations of state regulations are corrected and the "stop placement" status is lifted.

Support Staff: Members of the nursing home staff who do not care for the residents directly, such as housekeeping and maintenance.

Survey Report: The document written by the State survey team listing the violations of the nursing home.

Tour Guide: The staff member who conducts your tour. This individual may be the administrator, director of nurses or a marketing representative.

Transfer: The act of moving from one surface to another. For instance, moving from a bed to a wheelchair.

Bibliography

1. "Some Physicians Grossed Over $1 Million From Medicare Patients In 1992"; *PT Bulletin;* 35:11; 1995.

2. Beverly Enterprises. *Rehabilitation Services Ancillary Handbook: Revisions 1991.* Fort Smith, AR. 1990.

3. Covert AB, Rodrequez T, Solom K: "The Use of Mechanical and Chemical Restraints in Nursing Homes". *Journal of American Geriatrics Society,* 1977; 25:85.

4. Ericson, L. L. OTR/L, Contributing Editor/Consultant. "Restraints in the Nursing Home Environment". *Physical Therapy Forum.* September 4, 1992.

5. Felsenthal Edward. "Jury Awards Rise for Improper Care of Elderly". *TheWall Street Journal.* 9-5-95.

6. Friedman, Tappan. "The Effect of Planned Walking on Communication in Alzheimer's Disease". *Journal of the American Geriatrics Society* 39:650-654, 1991.

7. Furrow, Johnson, Jost, and Schwartz. *Health Law:Cases, Materials, and Problems.* St. Paul, MN: West Publishing Company, 1991.

8. Glickstein, JoanK. PhD and Neustadt, Gail K. MA. *A Functional Maintenance Therapy System: Reimbursable Geriatric Service Delivery.* Gaithersburg, MD: Aspen Publishers, Inc. 1992.

9. Green, Kathleen M. PT. "Malpractice Issues in Physical Therapy:. *Physical Therapy Forum.* March 1993; pp. 4-5.

10. Hausken, Greg PT and Winter, Patricia PT. "Changes in HCFA Survey for Skilled Nursing Facilities". *WSPTA Newsletter.* August 1995. P.11.

11. Hoffenreffer, Demetria P. and Gold, Marla Gern. "The Rewards of Restorative Care." *Provider*; Dec. 1991.

12. *Illustrated Stedman's Medical Dictionary*. Baltimore MD:Williams & Wilkins. 1982.

13. Schnelle, D. R. Newman, T.E. Fogerty, K. Wallston, N. Ory. "Assessment and Quality Control of Incontinence Care in Long-Term Nursing Facilities". *Journal of American Geriatrics Society*, 39:165-171, 91.

14. Lipsitz, et al. "Causes and Correlates or Recurrent Falls in Ambulatory Frail Elderly". *Journal of Gerontology Medical Science*, 46:M114-122, 1991.

15. May, Kenneth. "Restraints and the Law". *Nursing Homes* 1989; 8:9.

16. Murray, Joan: "Teamwork Made This Restraint-Reduction Program Work." *Advance* 1990; 16:14.

17. *New Webster's Dictionary of the English Language*. New York, NY: Delair Publishing Company, Inc.

18. NovaCare, Inc. *Restorative Nursing & Self Help Program*. Valey Forge, PA: S.E. Rehab Services. 1986.

19. *Nursing Home Charges in Florida: Intrd.* http://wane5.scri.fsu.edu/AHCA/NURSDAT/engnar95.html.

20. Orth, Ronelle. "Restorative Dining Promotes Independence, Self Esteem." *Provider*; December 1991.

21. Smith and Kaluzy. *The White Labyrinth: A Guide to the Health Care System*. Ann Arbor, MI: Health Administration Press, 1986.

22. Department of Health and Human Services Annual 1991: *Guide to Choosing a Nursing Home*. (Pamphlet)http://www.cognito.com/0004/articles/00014-022/14022683.htm.

23. Werman HM, Ovear ME: "Aalls and Restraints in a Skilled Facility." *Journal of American Geriatrics Society* 1986;34:907.

INDEX

HEALTH AND WOMEN-RELATED BOOKS

THE AIDS READER Documentary History of a Modern Epidemic By Loren Clarke and Malcolm Potts. ISBN 0-8283-1918-9 $17.95.

ALZHEIMER'S--A Handbook for the Caretaker by Eileen Driscoll. 2nd Printing. ISBN 0-8283-1962-6. $12.95 p.

With several decades of nursing experience, Eileen gives hope to those having to cope with alzheimer patients.

AUTISM--From Tragedy to Triumph by Carol Johnson and Julia Crowder. Illustrated. 2nd Printing 1996. ISBN 0-8283-1965-0 $12.95 p.

Carol and Julia tell the story of a young man, from birth to college matriculation--how Julia, the mother, coped with his illness.

BREAST CANCER AND YOU: BETTERING THE ODDS by Martha L. Grigg. Trade paperback, illustrated. ISBN 0-8283-2010-1, $14.95.

One woman in eight faces breast cancer and must make a choice about her treatment, her figure, and her future. Martha Grigg gives women the up-to-date information they will need to make treatment choices with the best odds for success. The book grew out of her own experiences, and the subject material ranges from the basic What Breast Cancer Is: Types and Staging, to treatment choices mastectomy versus lumptectomy, radiation, adjuvant chemotherapy, tamoxifen to coping, dealing with fear, finding support systems, and, of course, what the current odds are for possible prevention or cure. Readers will also find the latest on tamoxifen, the controversial but most prescribed cancer drug in the world.

MANUFACTURE OF BEAUTY by Ruth Kanin. Trade Paperback. ISBN 0-8283-1934-0 $12.95.

Ruth analyzes the industry that has and continues to regulate the standards and applications for the *beautiful* much to the detriment of women (and of men) who subject themselves to recurrent standardization.

PUMPKIN--A Young Woman's Struggle with Lupus by Patricia Fagan. ISBN 0-8283-1961-8 $12.95 p.

Patricia, the mother of *Pumpkin* is a professional nurse who more than just looked after her daughter.

PARKINSON'S A Personal Story of Acceptance by Sandi Gordon. Trade Paperback. Illustrated. ISBN 0-8283-1949-9 $12.95.

VISIT OUR PAGE ON THE INTERNET--www.branden.com